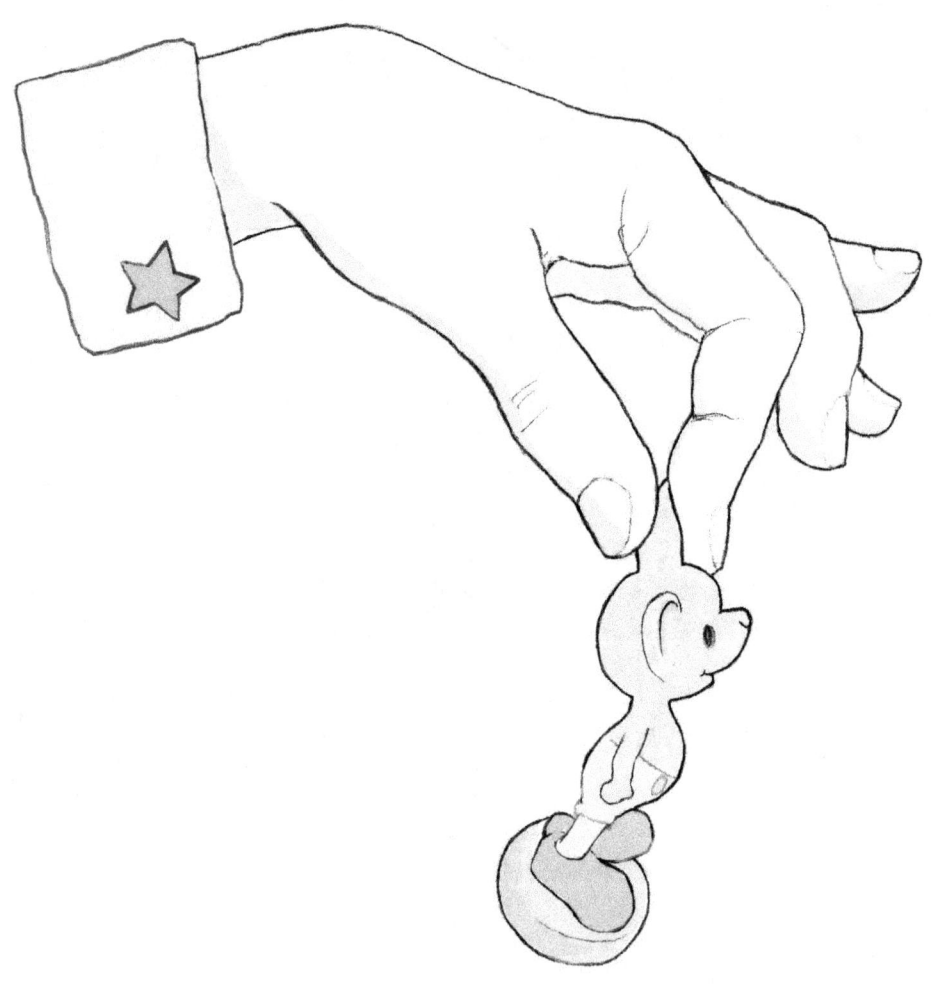

RHYMES and DOODLES from

A WIND-UP TOY

by
Martha Sears West

Clean Kind World
Los Angeles

Copyright © 2020, 2019 by Martha Sears West · Distributed by Ingram Book Company
Rhymes and Doodles from a Wind-up Toy. All rights reserved.
Library of Congress Control Number 2012953734
ISBN: 978-0-9886784-4-6(softbound); 978-0-98886784-0-8 (casebound)
CleanKindWorldBooks.com   ParkPlacePress.com   ymaddox@CleanKindWorldBooks.com
Toll Free 800·616·8081 · Shipping 435·764·4545 · Fax 323·953·9850
2016 Cummings · Los Angeles CA 90027
All titles are available online and in fine bookstores.
The Hetty series is available in print, audio, and eBook.
Jake, Dad and the Worm· Longer Than Forevermore · Rhymes and Doodles from a Wind-up Toy
Hetty · Hetty Happens · Hetty or Not · Honeymoon Summer · Hetty on Hold

10 9 8 7 6 5 4 3
Printed in the United States of America

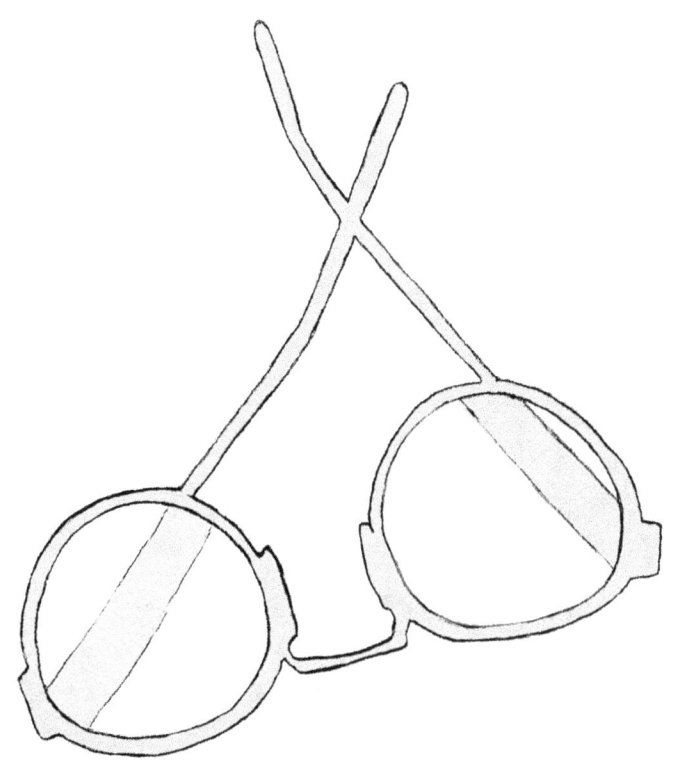

Dear Reader,
I appreciate parents, siblings, and dear friends and family who are happenmakers.
My deepest thanks Allan, Page, Adam, and their choice spouses and families. Special gratitude goes to my husband, Steve, for fifty-two years of creating memories, and for his gift of encouragement. These words at play are intertwined with my love. I hope they give you pleasure.

M.S.W.

POETIC SENSE

After reading poetry,
    I want to ask from whence
The poet found so many words
    That make so little sense.

This seems a rare frustration
    That I suffer all alone:
If I'm to understand a poem,
    I'll have to write my own.

I AM NOT A WIND-UP TOY

    I am not a wind-up toy;
        I do the things I choose.
    No one makes me squeak and spin
        In purple dancing shoes.
    No one winds a key that makes me
        Ride a little bike
    With pantaloons and parasol.
        No, I do what I like.

I think I got my pants on wrong,
    By dressing in a hurry.
Oh, well, I'll wear them inside out.
    I'm not going to worry.
But…flashing past a mirror…
    Could that image be my own?
A jaunty tag pokes stiffly
    From the seam where it was sewn.

I seem to have a wind-up key
    Protruding from my seat!
The mirror shows me as I am;
    The lesson is complete.
Even when I think that I'm
    The one in charge of me,
Conditions out of my control
    Are winding up my key.

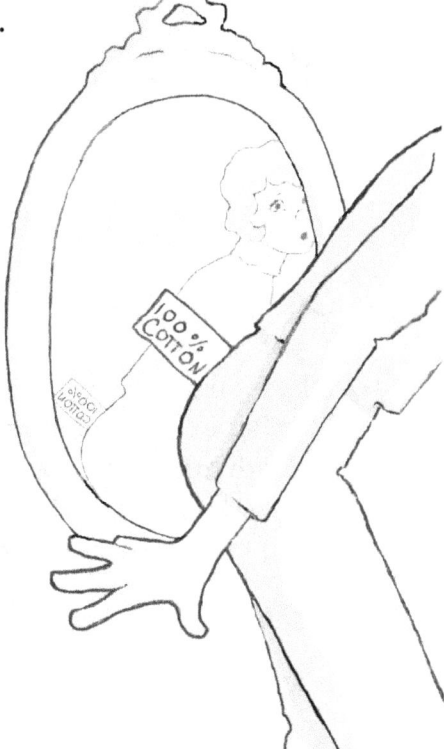

OSTRICH OF THE IMAGINATION

About the ostrich:
    All these years, I've simply been misled;
He doesn't dig a dirt hole
    To obfuscate his head.

The book that says he does,
    When he is hiding from a predator,
Should've been checked over
    By the scientific editor.

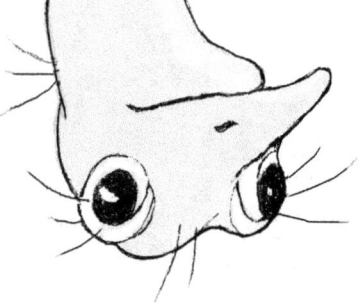

GOOSE ON THE LOOSE

What could possibly be the excuse
For a vicious, irascible goose
    With manners atrocious,
    And hissing ferocious,
Biting me on the caboose?

CRITTERS

Many living things we do admire.
Some we swat.

We may be created equal.
They are not.

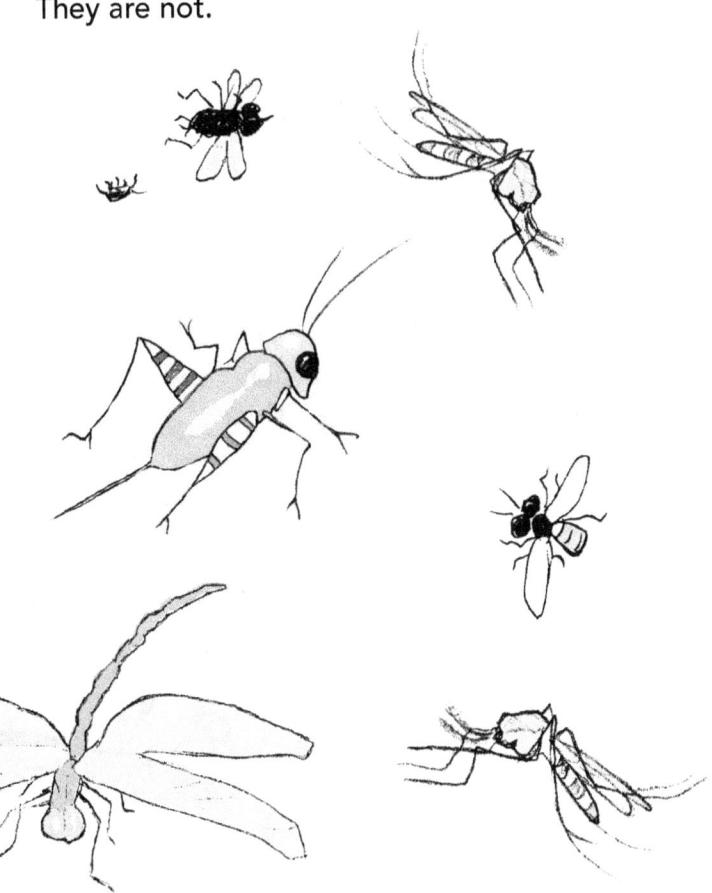

VETERINARY EMERGENCY

When Santa's disorganized elf
Left a choc'late bar low on the shelf,
    "They've gone," Maggie thought,
    "So I'll never get caught,
If I gulp it down all by myself!"

They got home to Maggie, and found
She was too weak to utter a sound;
    Lying curled in a ball,
    Chocolate, tinfoil and all,
As if ready to lay in the ground.

She was raced to the vet, in a cab,
(With what evidence someone could grab).
    "Oh, no need to bury her,"
    The vet said, "your terrier
Thinks she's a Chocolate Lab."

PETS

People tend to love their pets,
    And I am no exception.
Some animals, however,
    Rule their owners by deception.

My neighbor thinks her pussycat
    Is such a little dear,
And yet its teeth and claws have got me
    Paralyzed with fear.

I guess she doesn't understand
    That nothing could be stranger
Than harboring a crazy pet
    That poses such a danger.

When she complained about my dog,
    I very nearly choked,
For my dear Fang will bite your leg
    Only when provoked.

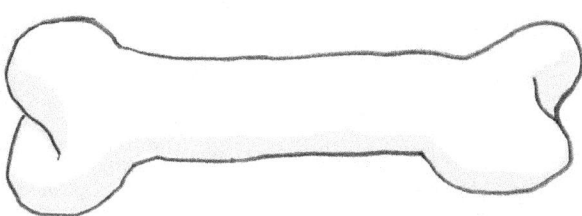

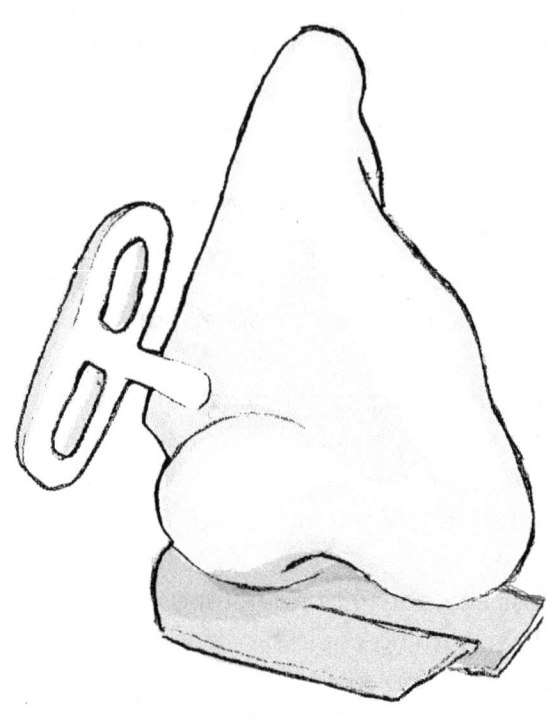

MY MECHANICAL NOSE

Unfortunate, the person
    Who sniffles, snorts or blows,
And has to mop with frequency
    A red and runny nose.

As for me, I've bought one
    With a guarantee behind it:
Its decorative nostrils will not run,
    Unless I wind it.

INCOMPATIBLE GUESTS

Cute little mousie, running through the housie,
I think we'd better show you to the door!
    You could end up in a trap
    With a quick and fatal snap,
And you wouldn't be so cute, anymore.

To our lovely dinner guest, you're a horrid little pest,
Darting like a furry shooting comet.
    The lady's looking pale
    Since she saw your little tail;
Oh, dear! I think she's going to…
              hurry home,
                 for she says she needs to
                 dust her houseplants.

WHO ATE MY CHAIR?

I accidentally kicked the ball
    Way up in a tree;
The branches were so thick and tall,
    I couldn't get it free.
To get it down, I figured
    I'd throw my brother's bat;
Now I guess the evergreen
    Is also keeping that.

I didn't think the little chair
    Would stay where it was thrown;
And sad to say, the ball's still there!
    Oh, how could I have known
So many things would end up lost,
    And never be of use
Because they accidentally tangled
    With a greedy spruce?

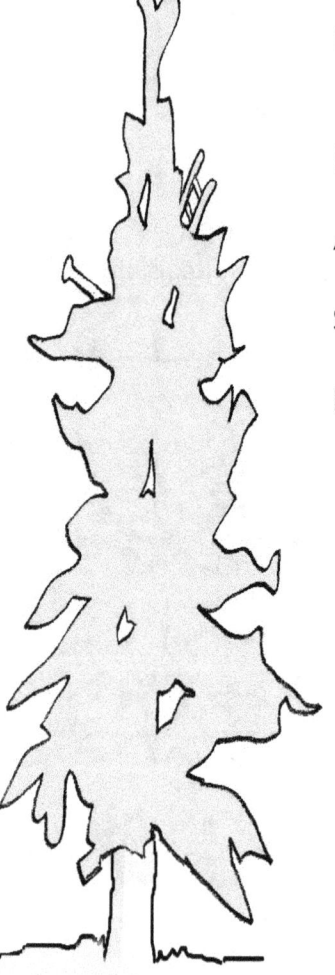

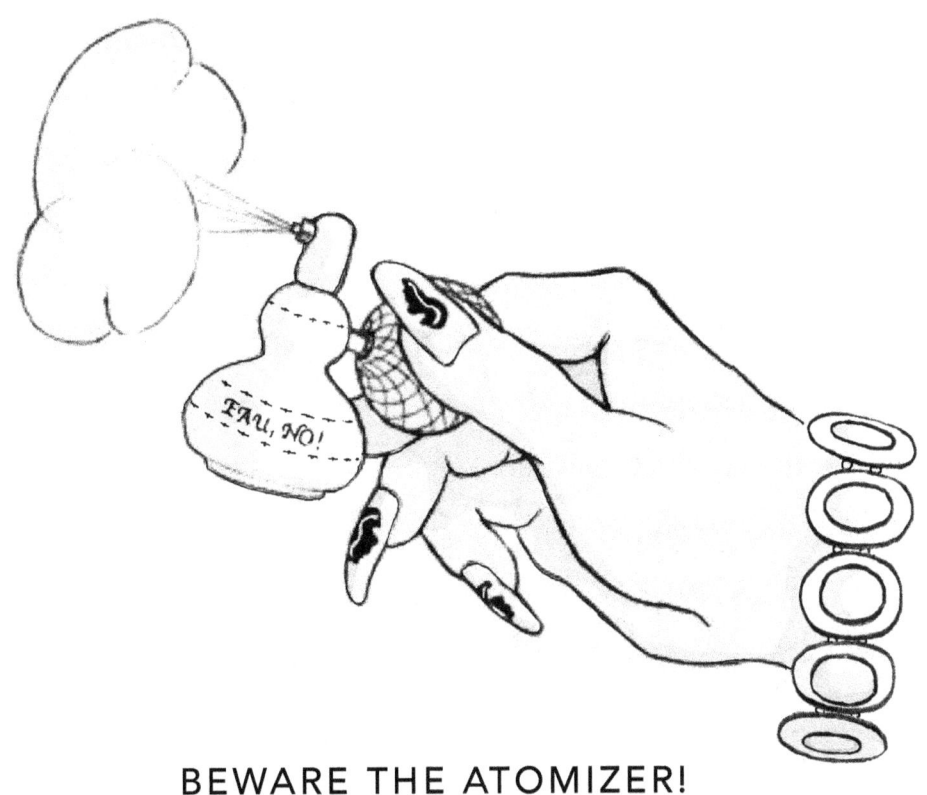

BEWARE THE ATOMIZER!

When entering
   The little French boutique,
I'm sprayed
   With perfume, costly and unique;
They'd save a lot,
   If someone ever thunk
I'd far prefer
   A dab of Eau de Skunk.

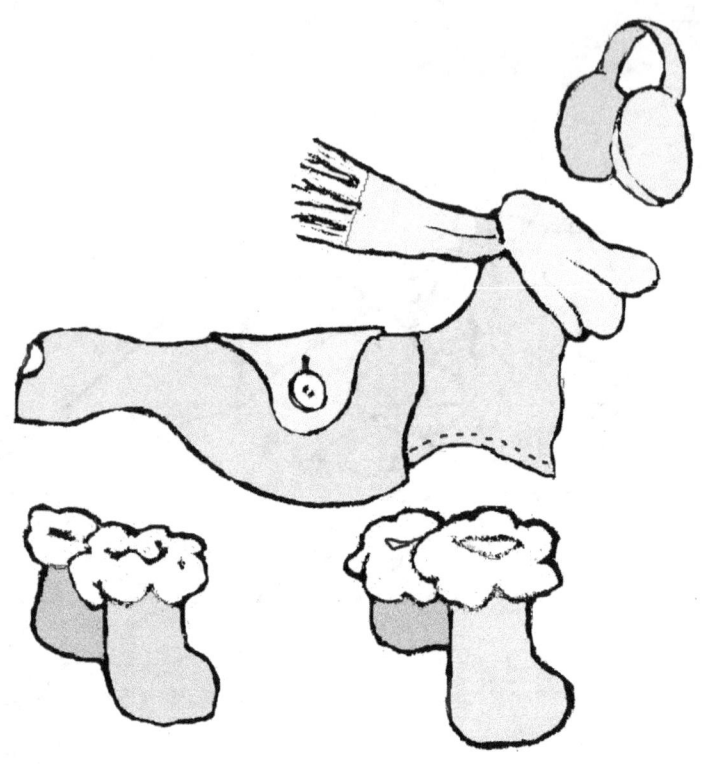

PUPPY CARE

Designed for
   Sunny Mexico,
He'll shiver and shake
   In the wind and snow,
With merely a fringe
   On his tail and snoot,
To accessorize
   His birthday suit.

So, cover your
   Mexican Hairless,
Who couldn't possibly
   Wear less.

NOW THEY KNOW

I said something sort of foolish,
    And feared they knew it was me;
So I hid my head in a paper bag...
    And walked into a tree.

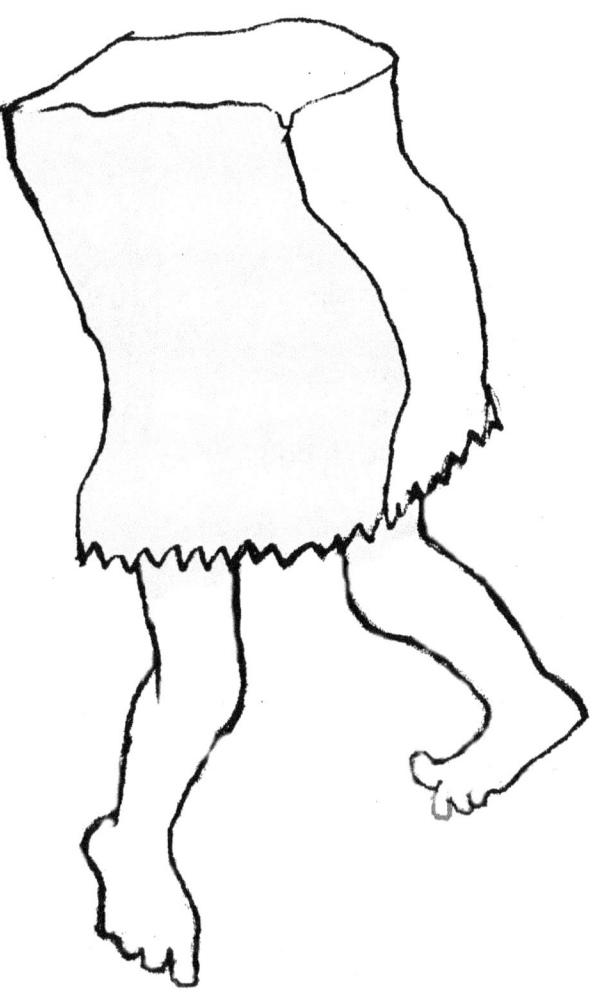

LOST IN TRANSLATION

Two men who were acquainted
    Saw each other in the park.
When the first one spied the other,
    He most cheerily said, "Hark!
How sun it is to fee you!
    It's been lutch a song, song time!
Your hife is wealthy? My, you
    Bared a snooty in your prime!

"I heard about the ladder
    She was cool enough to flime.
I hope she'll soon be better,
    That was surely crutch a sime!
It's so sad the lainty dady
    Has so much she's throwing goo!
Procure the dinest foctors;
    That's the diggest thing to boo.

"If you can't afford a doctor,
    Or a nurse to pet her gills,
Or lix the broken fadder…
    Oh, how do you air your bills?
I have trig bubbles, much like you;
    I'm in a picky trickle!
I doubt you have the dimmest slime.
    But can you spare a nickel?

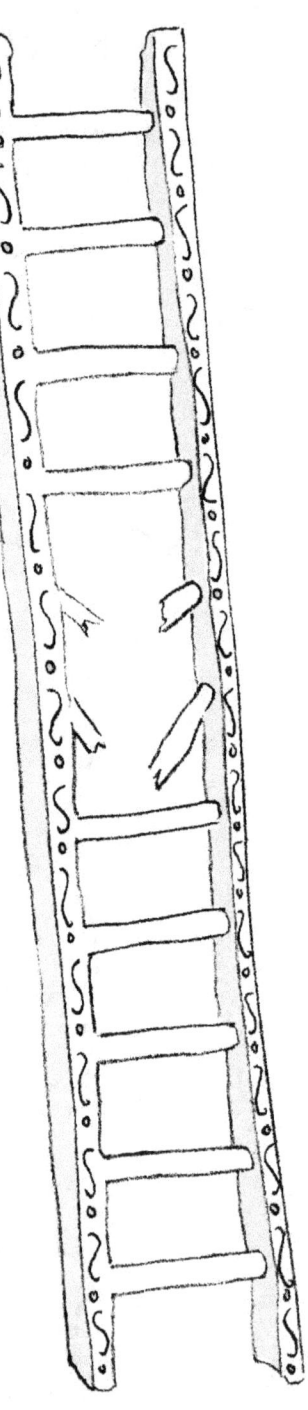

The other said, "Oh, dear,
 I didn't comprehend a word!
Young man there—were you listening?
 Can you tell me what I heard?"

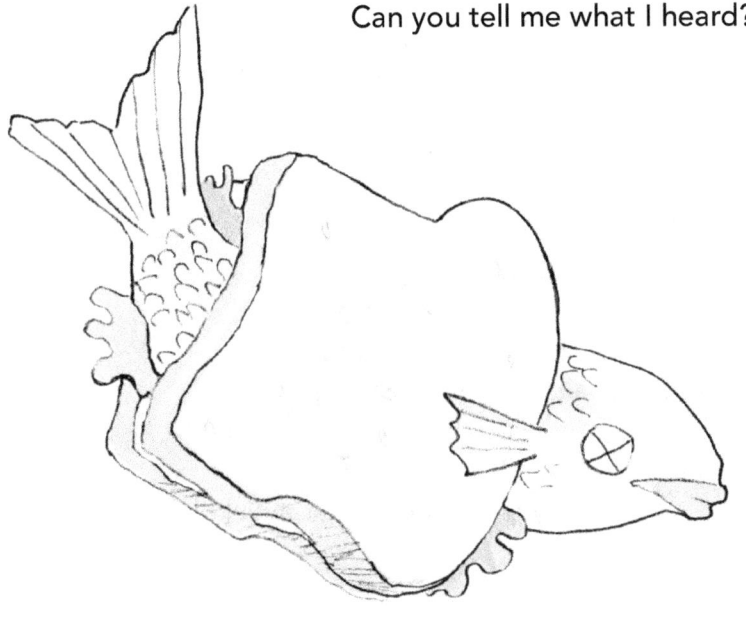

The boy at hand said, "Yes, I heard
 While sibling on my nandwich;
I'll translate what he said to you,
 For I can leak his spanguage.
Your friend is glad to see you,
 After such a long, long time.
He hopes the lovely wife you snared
 Will never pass her prime! 👉

"He knew about some ladder she was
    Fool enough to climb,
(And here it wasn't clear to me,
    The nature of her crime.)
He regrets the dainty lady
    Has such trials she's going through,
And suggests that getting doctors
    Should be mainly up to you.

"If you can't afford a doctor
    Or a nurse to get her pills,
Or fix that broken ladder,
    How he wonders at your ills!
He speaks of many troubles,
    For like you, he's in a pickle,
And he hasn't got a dime.
    (Oh, my translations cost a nickel.)

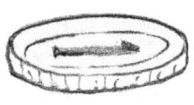

Now the storal of the mory:
    If you're throwing goo so much,
Plan on eeking spinglish,
    Or it's hard to keep in touch.
And sissoning with limpathy
    To hatters of your money
Does not excuse the go-between
    For milching any funny.

I AM WOMAN, HEAR ME SNORE

I was wondering how I could douse
The snoring that came from my spouse.
    The kids never slept,
    Except when we kept
The doors closed all over the house.

So I thought I should stay up and try
To watch him all night, as a spy.
    And when they reported,
    "Last night, no one snorted!"
I knew that the culprit was I.

YOUR CUP

Ants at the picnic, and gum on your shoes;
The thing that you need is the one that you lose.

Your pizza has anchovies; apples have holes;
The flower garden is riddled with moles.

Your motor breaks down when the warranty's up.
Your glass is half empty. You want a full cup!

But you dust yourself off and dress up in a smile,
Which feels pretty good, if you wear it a while.

Then you start a new day with a song and a prayer,
And pass out anchovies; it's nicer to share!

RHYME TIME

Here's a poem for you to read
    With a ditty in it:
(Just wait for me to think one up;
    It shouldn't take a minute.)

I told you I'd compose a rhyme,
    And so I thought I should.
In fact, it's what you're reading now.
    I wondered if you would.

THE FISHERMAN

The suffering of fishermen
Whom no one will believe
Is something of which other folks
Can't readily conceive.

Concerning the above frustration,
Here we give an illustration:

A man who'd swum out to a shoal,
　　While holding up his fishing pole,
Was gazing at the sea around,
　　When suddenly, without a sound,
There appeared two nonconformist
　　Devil Rays that were enormous!
Glistening in black and white,
　　Like blinding snow and inky night,
They rose from underneath a wave.
　　Unlike other fish behave,
They flew so high they hid the sun!
　　The man did just as you'd have done:

He sought a witness to enroll,
    (Like someone on the Beach Patrol).
But finding he was all alone,
    With rod aloft, he swam for home.
Inside the door, berserk and dripping,
    He sputtered out his tale most gripping:

"Two fish as big as our garage!
    Or maybe like a Travelodge!
"Gleaming there in black and white,
    Like blinding snow and inky night.
I've never seen around these parts
    Any fish so off the charts!"

His fam'ly, as he effervesced,
    Were quite polite, but unimpressed.
This tale he couldn't wait to tell
    Was not accepted very well.
Although they smiled and winked, delighted
    Just to see him so excited,
Still they doubted all he stated.
    Surely he prevaricated!

In later years, you'll never guess
    What thing arrived at their address:
A most amazing magazine!
    For all to see, on page eighteen,
A Devil Ray of mammoth size,
    Before the camera, up and flies!
This graceful fish's giant span
    Was being ridden by a man!
They said, "You have been vindicated,
    By a picture, though belated!"

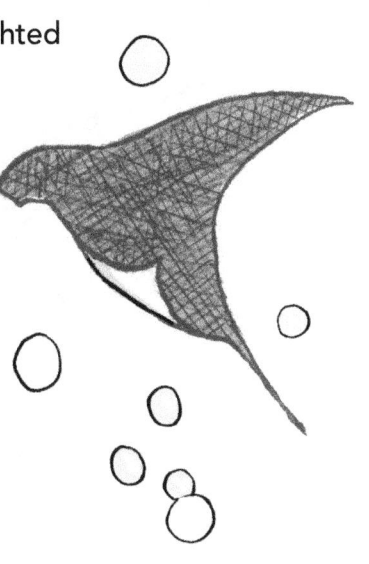

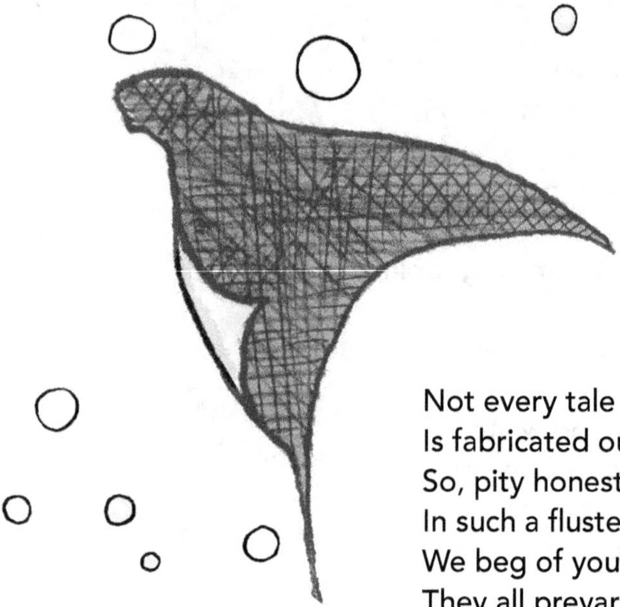

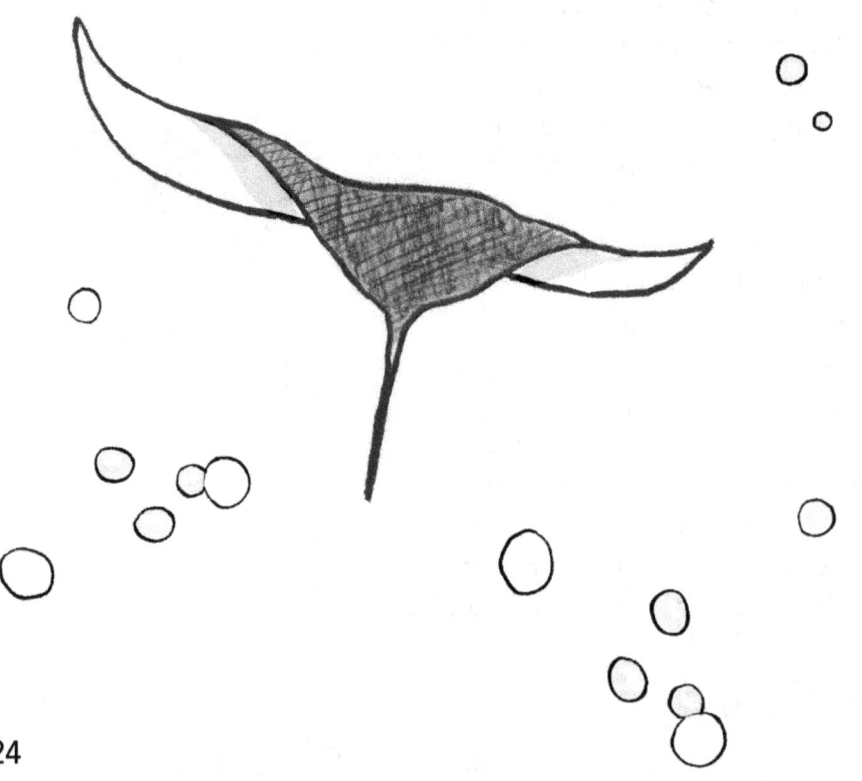

Not every tale that sounds unreal
Is fabricated out of zeal.
So, pity honest fishermen
In such a flustered state.
We beg of you, do not assume
They all prevaricate.

Thus we end our illustration
Of a fisherman's frustration.

GONE

It's little consolation,
 Now that all my hair is gone,
To know I sport the scalp
 That it was formerly upon.

WHY WE EXERCISE

If I were worse at any sport,
I guess I'd be on life support.

Indeed, I doubt that I'll arrive
At my own funeral much alive.

INTRODUCTORY PIANO LESSON

I'm so glad to be your
teacher. Howdy-do !
My piano's waiting eagerly for you.
    There's no reason to be frightened,
    And I hope you'll feel enlightened
When I've taught your little digits what to do.

Now to summarize my method, at a glance:
The arms should always undulate and dance.
    Half the keys should be caressed,
    Then karate all the rest.
You can leave the notes entirely to chance.

When both your hands are perfectly combined
With neither lollygagging much behind,
    May I suggest you oughta
    Raise a brow at each fermata-
A nicety that's ever so refined.

You should play it kind of dreamy-eyed at first,
With wistful little sighs interspersed.
    Toss your head for the finale,
    But don't forget, by golly,
To make it seem completely unrehearsed.

LAURA LEE

I long to gaze
    Into the dreamy eyes of Laura Lee;
Whenever I approach, withal,
    She shies away from me.
She'll never deign to speak her thoughts,
    Nor curtsey when I bow,
For Laura Lee, if truth be told,
    Will always be a cow.

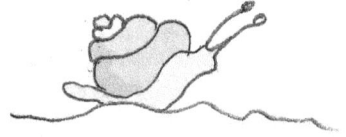

LOST EMAIL

Email messages
    Race through the air
Out in space,
    Who knows where!

They circle about
    In Saturn's rings,
With luggage we've lost
    And other things.

Like my grandparents
    Used to do,
I'm using a mailbox
    Hitherto.

WHAT NOT TO DO

Her tresses were blowing,
    But she didn't care
That her bonnet, and whatnot,
    Remained on the stair.

 Though she ought to have knotted
    Her hair in a comb,
She'd neglected to do it
    While she was at home.

So bluebirds and whatnot
    Made nests in her hair,
As she lay in the meadow,
    Enjoying the air.

The moral of what
    I've related to you
Should serve as a warning of
    What not to do.

VISITORS

I got my dollhouse ready,
    But the fairies never came.
I checked it every morning,
    And it always looked the same.
I thought they'd like it right away,
    If they should fly across
The dancing ring I made for them,
    With puffy velvet moss.

Hidden in a secret place,
    Beneath a lacey fern,
I left it there for quite a while,
    Just hoping they would learn
That I could be a gentle friend,
    And leave them quite alone.
I wouldn't peek, or tend the grass
    If it was overgrown.

Then suddenly, one day, when I had
    Left them to themselves,
My little house was visited
    By very naughty elves.
Perhaps a clumsy friend of theirs,
    Whose manners weren't so good,
Forgot to tidy up the rooms
    The way a fairy would.

A fiddlehead was broken,
    And nuts were all around.
Inside, the house was all upset;
    The bed was upside down.
Footprints smeared the attic roof,
    Which definitely proved
That someone really monstrous
    Must have been the one who moved
The polka dotted tablecloth,
    Now hanging from the gate,
And eaten both the huckleberries
    On the china plate.

The house is in my bedroom now,
    Where I can guard the place.
You can't depend on fairies;
    I'll be watching, just in case.

SUNRISE

I rustle in the bed of leaves
    That warmed me through the night,
And stretch in my pajama sleeves,
    Blinking at the light
To watch the brilliance of the sun,
    And golden sky, unfurled,
Revealing miracles begun
    Upon the dewy world.

What the..? Where..? My tent is gone!
    Every rope and pole?
Oh, there it is, by light of dawn,
    Beside a rabbit hole!
How many little birds and frogs
    Have seen it crumpled there,
And puzzled, sitting on their logs,
    At such a silly lair?

I bumble, gawking at the day,
    As creatures all around
Join the laughter of the jay.
    Then, echoing the sound,
Cheerfully, they seem to call,
    "We're glad it blew away,
For sunrise can't compare at all,
    With humans on display."

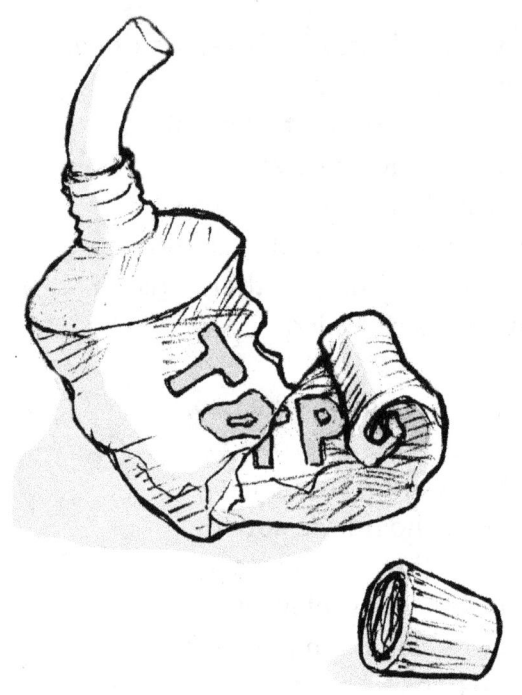

LITTLE TOMMY TOOTHPASTE

When we were tucked in bed at night,
    Our father used to say, "Let's see..."
Which meant, "A story's coming."
    Sure as it could be!

He'd tell us of a hero,
    Whose middle name was Tommy;
A lot of people squeezed him,
    But he didn't have a mommy.
Carelessly abandoned
    Beside a broken comb,
His owner didn't miss him,
    Until returning home.

Tommy joined a circus act,
    Performing very well.
What courage, for a toothpaste tube
    Left in some hotel!
He scuffled once with tigers,
    Who threatened him with death,
But credits his survival to
    His fresh and minty breath.

Though Tommy, with the passing years,
    Did not get any newer,
And sadly, inner parts of him
    Were washed into the sewer,
Still, he never did forget
    To doff his cap politely
In honor of the gentleman
    Whose teeth he polished nightly.

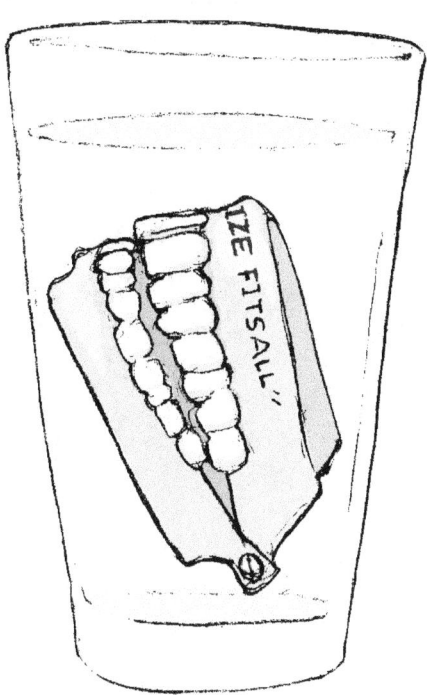

STEWED PRUNES

Prunes have often been maligned
By those who think them less refined.
    They're really very tasty!
So, if you thought they were reserved
For nursing homes where they are served,
    Your judgment may be hasty.

They're lovely strewn with pumpkin seed;
Extraordinary fricasseed.
    I always keep some near!
Each prune's a conversation piece,
So, should discussion ever cease,
    I place one in my ear.

Arrange them on a silver platter,
(Any size, it doesn't matter)
    With a lobster canapé.
For company, a special touch:
Garnish them with mint and such,
    Then throw the prunes away.

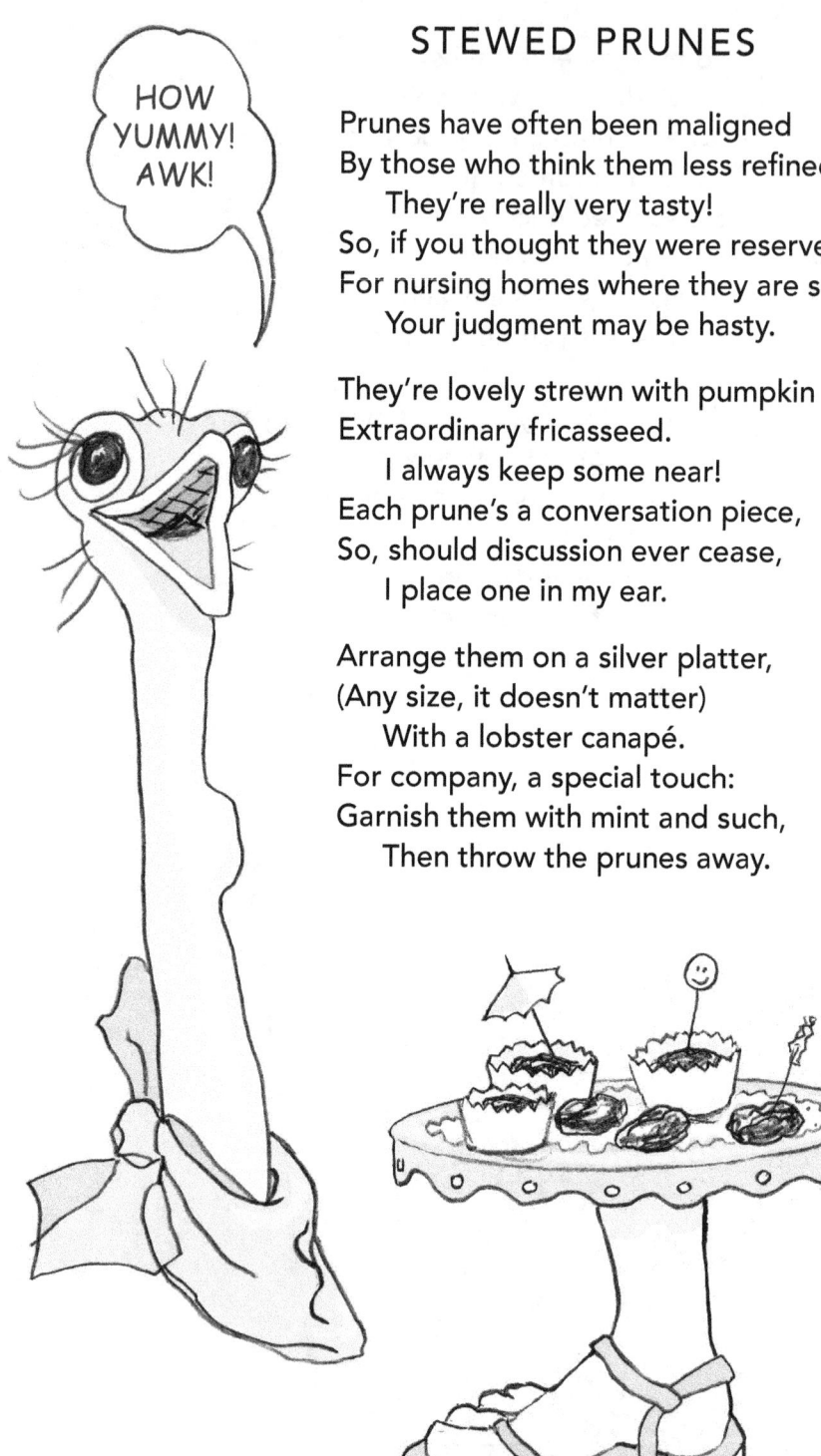

ONCE UPON A HAPPY TIME

Once upon a long ago,
    Was life all fun and laughter?
Did folks do all they wished to do,
    Happily ever after?

And was it like the fairy tales?
    Let's see… how do they go?
Were three blind mice in the house of straw,
    When the wolf began to blow?
Did Simple Simon kiss the frog,
    As the queen jumped over the moon?
When Little Boy Blue up the London Bridge,
    Did the prince run away with the spoon?
Was Little Red Riding a pumpkin coach?
    Did Cinderella fall?
Or was it Humpty Dumpty
    Who was dancing at the ball?

When Mother wants to tell them right,
    Go get the book, and let her!
From tales like these, you may decide
    That living now is better.

THE BEST CHRISTMAS

For Christmas, won't you take my hand
    The way you used to do?
I've seen the wonders of sea and land,
    And I want to be with you.

We'll go to a place we've been before;
    What a Christmas it will be!
We'll dance in the kitchen, one time more,
    If you will come for me.

I CAN FLY

It may appear I'm sleeping, and do you wonder why?
    I'm joyously imagining how it is to fly!
Soundlessly, I'm hovering above the frothy sea,
    Graceful as the pelican gliding next to me.
Soaring in the seamless sky, with heaven everywhere,
    Beams of sunshine playing in the tangles of my hair…

I close my eyes to memorize the softness of the breeze,
    And reach beyond the shards of light with open hands, to seize
The brilliance of a rainbow, between my fingertips,
    As droplets of a wispy cloud distill upon my lips…
But if you see me nodding, or sliding off the chair,
    I've simply met with turbulence, in such a lot of air!

When there's a smile upon my face, I haven't lost my mind;
    I'm just an eagle, happily observing humankind…
Soaring through the seamless sky, with heaven everywhere,
    Then diving for a silver fish that hasn't got a prayer!
If the cup I'm holding should tumble to the floor,
                       It means that for the moment,
                       I'm not flying anymore.

NOT THAT BEDTIME STORY!

The tale of John and Nory's short,
However, it's the one
That everybody wants to end,
Before it has begun.

Sometimes, Dad will tell it
As he tucks us in our beds.
We always cry, "Not that one, please!"
And cover up our heads.

Our dad can say it faster
Than a fish can even sneeze,
But till he tells a better one,
It's fun to hear him tease:

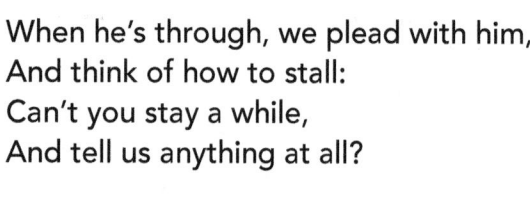

"I'll tell a story 'bout John and Nory,
    And now my story's begun.
I'll tell another 'bout John and his brother,
    And now my story is done."

When he's through, we plead with him,
And think of how to stall:
Can't you stay a while,
And tell us anything at all?

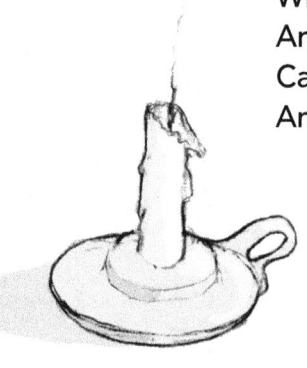

Then he turns the lights off,
So we can see the moon,
While singing words he's making up
To some familiar tune:

"'Twas only an old juice bottle,
  A-floating on the foam.
A very old juice bottle,
  So far away from home.
Inside was a piece of paper,
  With these words written on:
'Whoever finds this bottle,
  Finds the juice all gone.'"

If we are not asleep by then,
We have to all pretend,
Or he repeats that dreadful
"John and Nory," in the end.

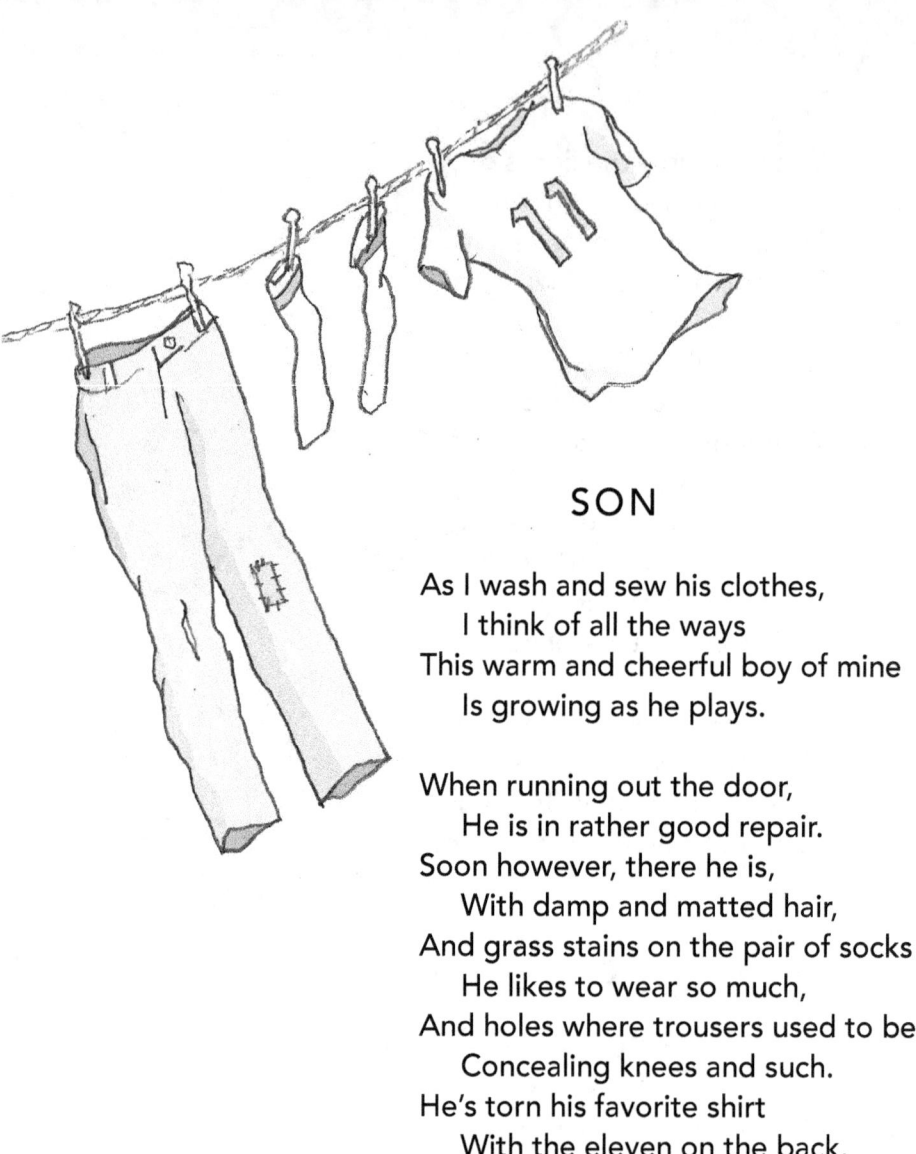

SON

As I wash and sew his clothes,
    I think of all the ways
This warm and cheerful boy of mine
    Is growing as he plays.

When running out the door,
    He is in rather good repair.
Soon however, there he is,
    With damp and matted hair,
And grass stains on the pair of socks
    He likes to wear so much,
And holes where trousers used to be
    Concealing knees and such.
He's torn his favorite shirt
    With the eleven on the back,
By skidding to the finish line,
    Along a racing track.

I wish the wife he'll have someday
    Could share with me the joy
Of knowing him, as I do now...
    This warm and cheerful boy.

FOREVERMORE

The weather changes often;
    So do hands upon a clock.
When warmth has changed to cold,
    We change to soft and wooly socks.

But one thing never changes
    And will last forevermore:
We'll love you still when you are grown,
    Exactly as before.

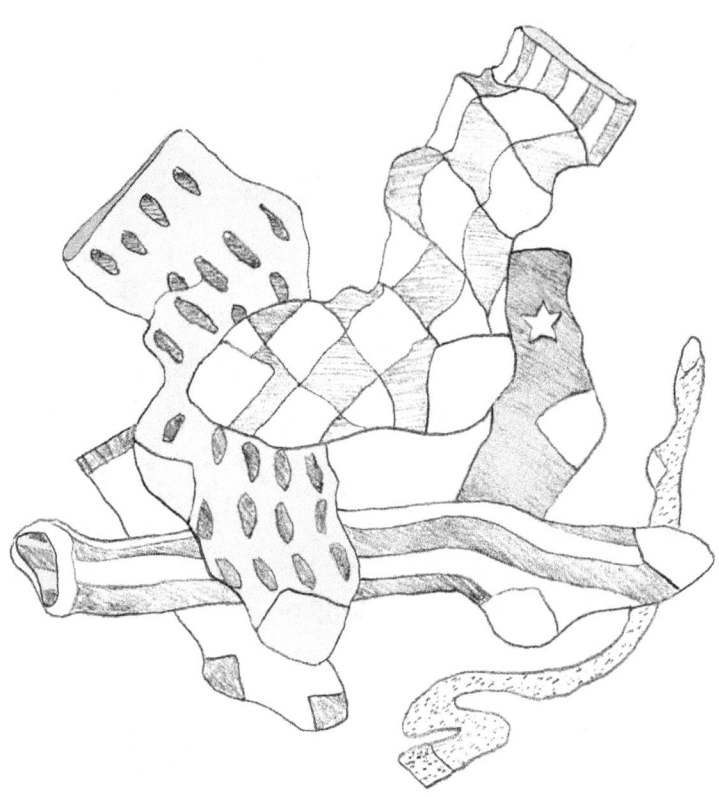

THE MEETING

Shall we meet in the garden today?
The squirrels will show you the way.
While lilacs stand guard
At the edge of the yard,
We'll watch the hummingbirds play.

THE WOOD

Deep in the heart of the wood,
The mighty oak tree stood.
And all 'round the edges,
The gooseberry hedges
Grew as well as they could.

THOUGHTS OF LOST LOVE

He met his sweetheart, Marigold,
    Along the river's side.
Her smile, so lovely to behold,
    Was famous, far and wide.

In his suave and witty way,
    He said to her, my love,
Pray, join me in the city
    And be my turtledove.

Kind was he, and debonair,
    But she replied, *I fear*
I cannot leave the river!
    Then shed a salty tear.

Now Marigold dispels her gloom
    By floating in the Nile,
And thinking of the groom
    Who might have walked her down the aisle.

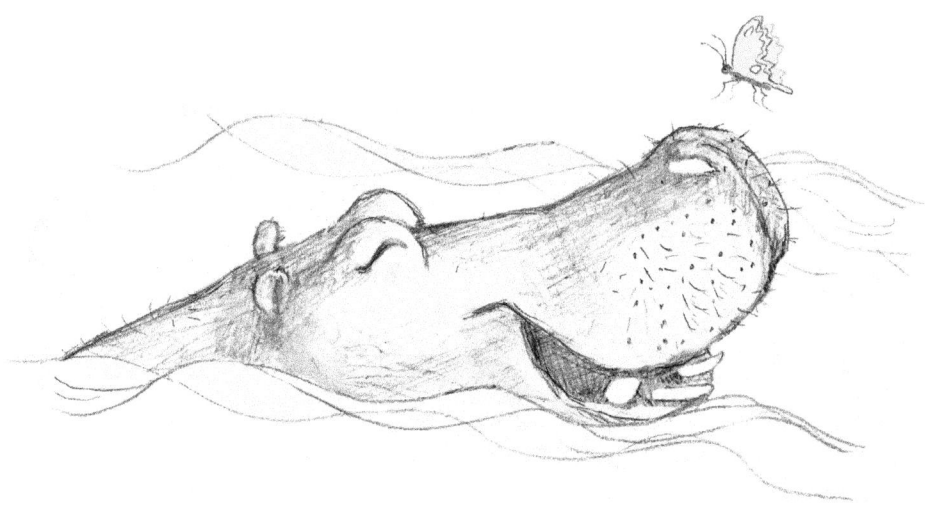

AN EAGLE

I wish I were an eagle
    In wild and wonderous weather,
Soaring, as the wind and rain
    Ruffle every feather.

I'd cross the English Channel;
    Look down at Paris, France,
And watch umbrellas carried
    By brightly colored ants.

I'd see the tempest raging
    Through field and open space;
Drenching sleepy villages
    And busy marketplace.

When the storm is over,
    And the sun sinks in the west,
Toward the Alpine cliffs I'd fly
    And settle in my nest.

NOTE ON A CABIN DOOR

The sheets are clean,
    The towels are out.
We've scrubbed around
    The water spout.
We hope you leave it
    As you find it.
If you can't,
    Then never mind it.
The privy's that way,
    Not too far.
Kindly leave the door ajar.

THE FLIGHT OF TIME

Hooray! Today won't come again!
    Unless it's what you call it when
Tomorrow comes while I'm in bed,
    With pillows covering my head.
Just like the past became today
    So fast, it's still in disarray,
The future's coming anyhow,
    Before I'm through with here and now.

MONKEY BUSINESS

The monkeys that sit on the wall
Have simply no manners at all.
    They pelt me with fruit
    And other such loot.
So, I carry a parasol.

They loll about on the roof,
And to tell the honest truth,
    I'm willing to share
    If they like it there,
But I wish they'd all go *poof!*

MAGIC

By kissing a frog, you get a prince,
But how do you get a king?
It won't occur, I'm quite convinced,
By kissing anything.

A TAD

A most enchanting princess
    Once kissed a royal frog,
And now she is expecting
    Their firstborn polliwog.

The kingdom is delighted
    Their prince will be a dad.
When asked if he is nervous,
    He answers, *just a tad.*

NEW, EASY-OPEN CONTAINER

I could make an endless list of foods I never ate
Because I couldn't open them by expiration date.

The modern-day container says: *sealed for your protection.*
  Please pull perforated tab in opposite direction.
Firmly twist the ring atop the lid as indicated.
  Heed the sell-by date and use before anticipated.
Do not shake excessively, due to carbonation.
  Do not place on open fire or puncture in frustration.

The vittles sitting on my shelf will have to wait until a
Chainsaw comes to help me out, or even a gorilla.

THE JUMPING BEAN

Of all the wonders we have seen,
    What could match the jumping bean?
Pyramids are never found
    To similarly hop around.

BY CAR

If wondering where you are
And why you walked so far
    With a miserable blister
    And broken transistor,
Next time, travel by car.

PHOOEY

A guy named Louie I knowed
Came to a fork in the road.
    The sign said how far
    From here to thar,
But not how far he had strode.

    Oh, phooey, said Louie.

ON FIRE

Once there was a naughty bloke
    Who wallowed in the mire.
And every time he spoke,
    He called someone else a liar.

He lived the law of tit for tat
    And, over time, became
So very good at lying
    That he set his pants aflame.

Now he sits in swarms of flies
    (He isn't very couth),
And spends his time producing lies
    While swatting at the truth.

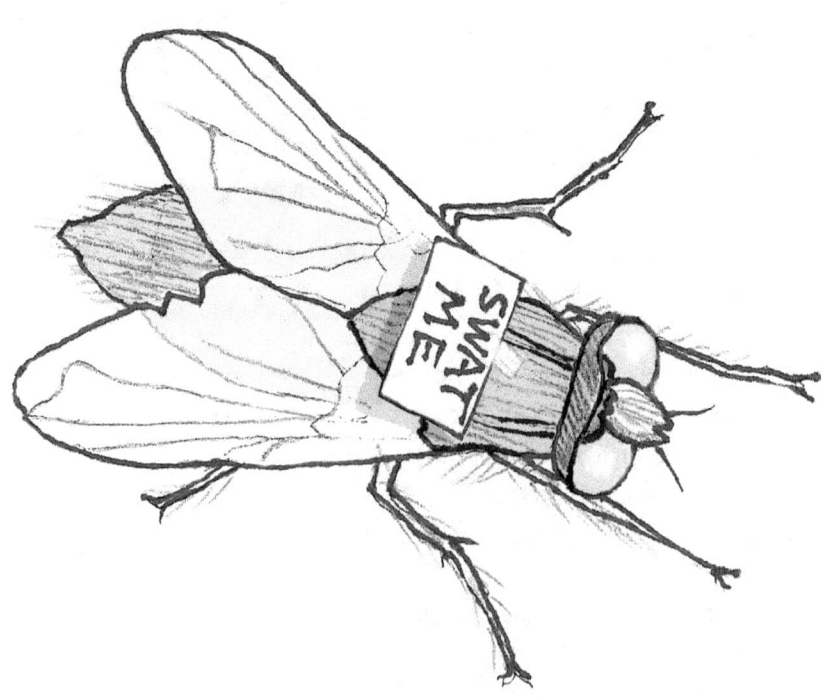

FAIRY CHILD

I wasn't born a fairy child;
    How lucky I was not!
I'd never gather teeth;
    I'd just enjoy the ones I've got.

I would gather acorn caps
    On yellow summer walks,
And tiny things I've made with you,
    To fill my secret box.

DORIS AND THE CHORUS

In the choir, they would never allow
People singing, who didn't know how,
    But since they've let Doris
     Just smile in the chorus,
It looks like they sound better, now.

DITTY SCHMITTY

A witty little ditty,
    Or a short sorta song
Wouldn't be pretty,
    If it went too long.
I'll tap my toes
    When a verse is terser.
The longer it goes,
    The more it's worser.

THE FATHER'S DAY GIFT

Father's Day's here! I've got something he'll like:
This thing that goes 'round and around, on a spike.
Whatever it is, I really can't say,
But I know that he needs it, anyway.

When I reached in my sock and I got out the money,
The lady who counted it, said to me, "Honey,
If you need a present to give to your pa,
Maybe some shaving cream…even a saw
Might be a regular gift, Little Miss."
She yelled to the manager, "Bruce, what is this?"
The manager answered, "Now, that's quite a sight!"
And the best thing of all, is I knew he was right!

I hardly can wait for my daddy to see
This thing that he's 'specially getting from me.
He'll give me the hugest hug and a kiss,
And I betcha he might even know what it is.

THE CHANGE OF PLANS

"Be a good boy, Son.
    And have a fun time."
"Bye, Mom," I said,
    (Thinking, "Make up your mind!")
I wasn't quite telling her
    All of my plans
To throw rotten apples
    And rusty tin cans.

I got to the tree,
    But my buddies weren't there,
And foul smelling apples
    Were everywhere.
Old Mister Smith,
    Working hard with a rake,
Winked, and asked,
    "How long you think it'll take?"

He says I'm a worker,
    And strong as could be!
And gave me the best apples
    Picked from the tree.

As I started to leave,
    He invited me back,
And his wife brought us cookies
    And milk for a snack.

"About those bad apples,
    We sure have a lot,
He said," and I bet
    You're a pretty good shot!
"Let's practice our aim,
    It can't do any harm!"
So we tossed just a few
    At the door of the barn.

Near home, I remembered,
    While picking up cans,
That I had completely
    Forgotten my plans!
"The apples are beautiful!
    What a good son."
I answered, "I love you, Mom.
    And I had fun!"

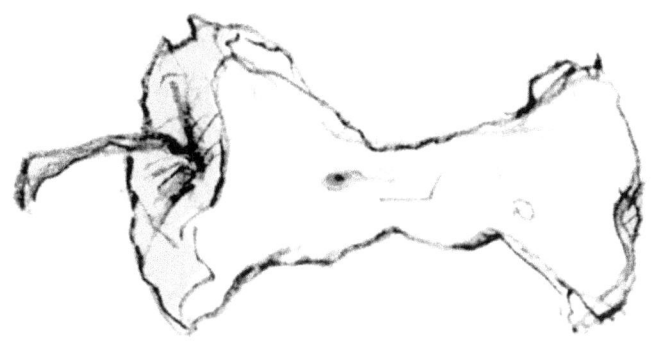

A GENTLEWOMAN

Julie earns,
    In kind and gentle ways,
Her friends' and loved-ones'
    Gratitude and praise.
With thanks, we join them all
    In saying truly,
We too are blessed because of
    Knowing Julie.

A WISE POINT

Here is Donna's wise decree:
    "Learn to pray at your mother's knee,
For we will not," she makes the point,
    "Learn at any other joint."

THE PLAYER PIANO

When Daddy puts a quarter
    In the fun pinanio,
I can spin in circles fast,
    And you can do it slow!

You can clap and cheer for me
    While I'm marching by,
Or when I'm swaying to and fro,
    Or jumping really high!

We can be like elephants
    Or dance on tippy-toe,
When Daddy puts a quarter
    In the fun pinanio!

I wonder why it doesn't need
    Some hands to make it play;
I'm glad, with no one there at all,
    It's working, anyway.

FAREWELL

The sad and precious time had come.
    My heart was with my son;
His plans would take him far from home,
    Till he was twenty-one.

He nevermore would be the same
    In intellect, or size.
Just knowing that he bore my name,
    Made tears come to my eyes.

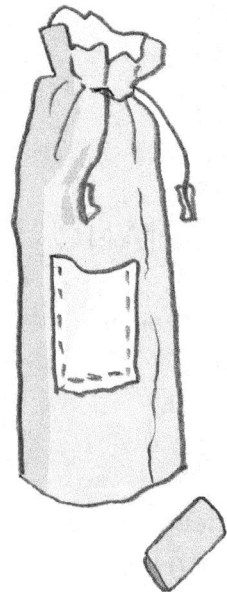

The time drew near. He asked if we
    Could take a little walk.
Perhaps he wanted privacy
    For this, our final talk?

He said, "So much I want to know,
    By hearing what you'll say!
I need advice before I go,
    I'll be so far away!

" A talk with you will help a lot,
    As always in the past.
This is something awkward, Dad.
    I hesitate to ask."

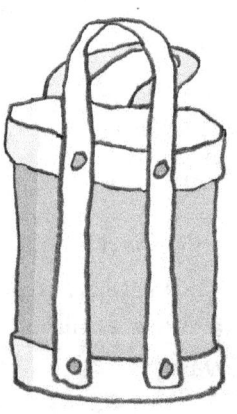

A rush of perspiration.
    A weakness in my knees.
Was now his time to ask me
    All about the birds and bees?

"It's awkward asking friends
    About what everybody knows.
My ignorance in this
    I'm quite reluctant to disclose:

"I've never had a haircut
    That wasn't done at home,
Since Mother is the only barber
    I have ever known.

"Would you explain the process,
    And what I should expect?
Just how do you decide
    Upon the barber to select?"

We laughed, and talked of tipping
    And defending both his ears.
In part, the talk was serving
    To alleviate my fears.

Until I learned Japan would be his home
    For twenty years.

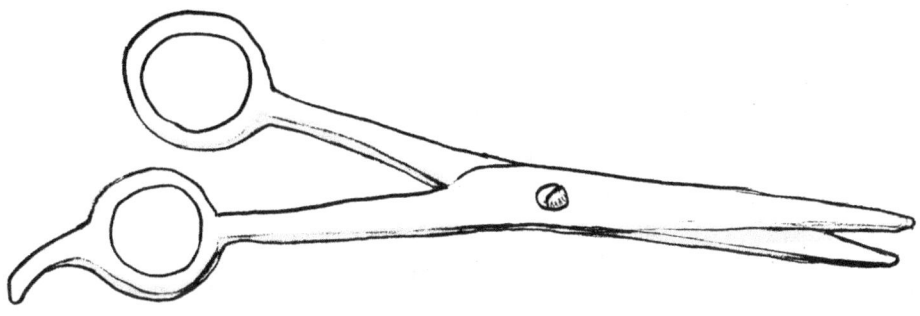

GRANDMOTHER

Grandmother says that long ago,
    She used to be my size.
But now she has a grownup face,
    With wrinkles 'round the eyes.
Once she had a tree house;
    I wish she had it now!
Still, we like pretending things,
    'Cause she remembers how.

BUTTERED TOAST

Grandma bakes the bestest bread!
    It smells throughout the house.
And when she tucks me into bed
    I'm quiet as a mouse,
Dreaming of tomorrow
    When she'll give me buttered toast.
Sleeping here at grandma's
    Is what I love the most!

AND SYRUP

When you make a johnnycake,
    It doesn't much matter
How the heck you mix it
    Or what's in the batter.

Cook it in the oven
    Or fry it in a pan,
But add all the lovin'
    And butter that you can.

WHAT YOU'LL NEED

When leaving home, it's good to plan
    Carefully indeed,
To get where you'll be living
    With everything you need.

You'll want to take a city map,
    A schedule for the bus,
Some books about the customs
    Of the local populace;
Addresses for the church, the school,
    And several stores and such;
A phone that will enable
    Folks back home to keep in touch;
A plan that helps you to enjoy
    (And maybe socialize)
With people whom you might not
    End up meeting, otherwise.

And most of all I wish for you,
    When at the other end,
That you can find and get to know
    A dear and helpful friend.

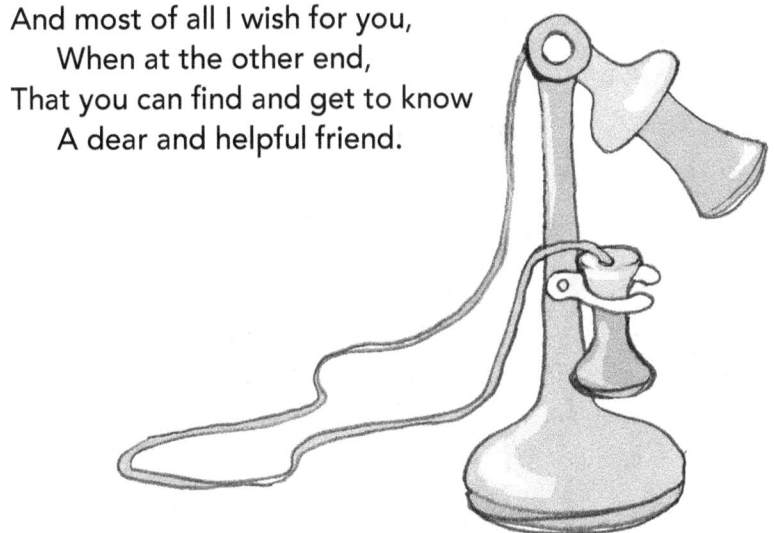

HAPPY BIRTHDAY TO ME

Every year, I'm older
    Than I was the year before;
Soon I'll need a big cake
    With many candles more.

What is big, you wonder?
    Well, Texas qualifies!
There a cake is just a crumb
    With icing for disguise.

A MESSAGE TO ANONYMOUS

Your kindness came in secret.
    So, I raise a prayer to heaven
That He'll convey my gratitude,
    If only you will listen.

And yet the dearest gift of all,
    I wish you'd realize,
Would be to speak my love and thanks
    While looking in your eyes.

FIDO FISH

I doubt if you are old enough
    To train a little puppy.
They bark, said Dad, *and chew on stuff,*
    So, how about a guppy?

Johnny wasn't sure at first.
    But when his guppy came,
He chose to call it Fido
    And loved it all the same.

John was quite responsible
    And walked it in the park,
So Dad gave him permission
    To teach Fido to bark.

FROM DAD

Try to guess what present
    I'm hiding in the attic
I got it for your birthday;
    This one's not aquatic.

It's got four legs; it chases balls
    And barks a lot, of course.
I absolutely promise
    It's not a flying horse.

The answer was so obvious,
    Johnny had to laugh.
He knew without a doubt
    It was not a blue giraffe.

It's black and white, begins with "D,"
    And rhymes with animation.
Johnny guessed it right.
    It was a dog named *Celebration*.

NO THANK YOU

Put me in a snake pit
    Or on a bed of nails;
I can face anchovies,
    And I'm rather fond of snails.

But even if I hold my nose,
    I'll never choose to risk
Injuring my taste buds with
    Norwegian lutefisk.

MY BLACK HOLE

I've crammed into my bulging purse a lot of useful stuff;
I'd put in more, to make it worse, if there were room enough!

>It's fairly bursting open,
>   With all I've squeezed within it:
>A tulip bulb, a top that has
>   Instructions how to spin it,
>Knitting needles, fabric samples,
>   Sundry baby clothes,
>A rather more than adequate
>   Supply of panty hose,
>A cane that folds to any size,
>   Some honey in a jar,
>Binoculars, 'cause otherwise
>   I couldn't see as far.

There's more than one of everything, which isn't even funny;
I'll never reach inside it, since I broke the jar of honey.

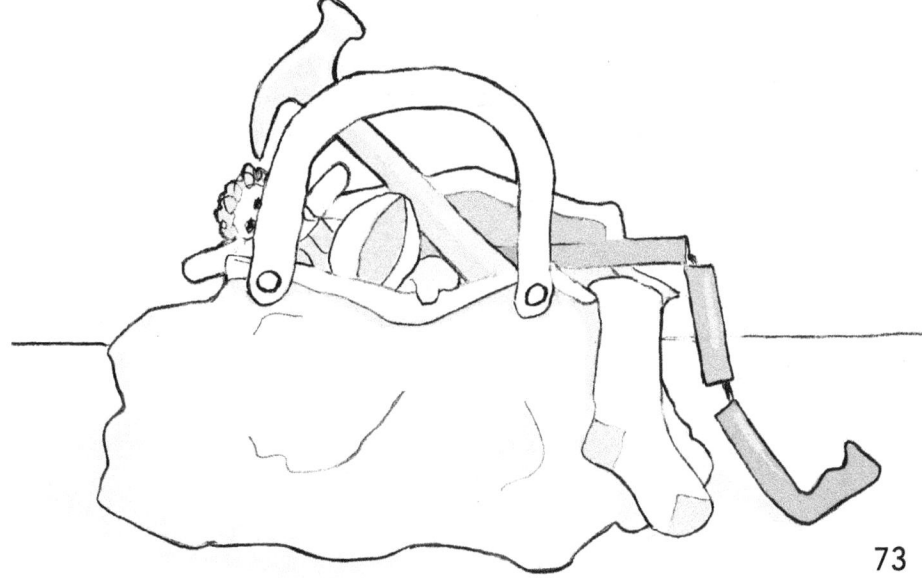

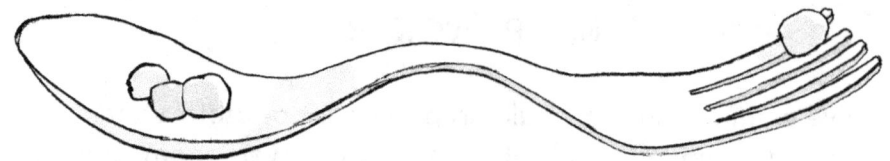

SUPPERTIME

Harry Watson grinned with joy
    At his every girl and boy,
While smells of supper in the air
    Gave promise of delicious fare.

To his wife, who waited there,
    Perched upon an oaken chair,
Harry crooned while sniffing dinner,
    "Dear, you've cooked another winner!
Such aromatic onion sauce!
    And I'll admit I'm at a loss
To adequately speak my praise
    Of such a lovely lemon glaze!"

With satisfaction, Harry smiled,
    And gathered up his youngest child.
He wiggled Adam's every toe,
    And thought he'd rather never go
To market as the piggy had,
    But stay at home and be a dad!
Fortunately, Allan chose
    To not put peas between his toes,
But found it just the time to start
    A mushy greenish work of art.

"Here's a joke, Dad," Lizzy said.
    "I keep a lot inside my head.
Here's the first. It's really neat:
    'Why did the chicken cross the street?'"
Her father said, "I must confess,
    I really couldn't hope to guess!"
With each successive clever riddle,
    Harry shook around the middle.
He turned quite pink, guffawed and quaked,
    Until his laughing muscle ached.
Content, he grinned again with joy
    At every little girl and boy.

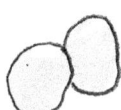

To show the very love of life,
    He danced a samba with his wife.
"Years ago, I never knew
    That I'd be here with all of you!
I wish forever you'd be there,
    Each seated in your special chair."

SNOWFALL

Twinkle, twinkle little flakes;
    Why are you, for heaven's sake,
Falling on the icy road,
    Confining me to my abode?

TO A CLAM IN MY CHOWDER

Twinkle, twinkle little clam,
    Do you wonder what I am?
As I thought, of course you don't!
    Now I promise that I won't
Keep conversing with my soup
    As if I were a nincompoop.

THE LATE SHOW

The Dumpletons were so polite
They never could decide
Whose turn it was for anything,
No matter how they tried.
What movie should we see, my dear?
Oh, you decide, my love.
Not before you tell me
Which one you're thinking of.

Tell me first, I must insist!
Which one would you select?
No, go ahead, my dearest!
And so, when last I checked,
The Dumpletons were still unsure
Which movie to attend.
In fact, I doubt they worked it out
Before the movie's end.

MAYBE AND ALONE

When Maynard Jones and Beatrice
Had a little baby,
They joined their names together,
And called their daughter "Maybe."

In time, a couple moved next door,
Called Alice and Tyrone.
They took the Jones' example,
And named their child "Alone."

One day, Alice asked,
"Oh, Bea, could Maybe tend Alone?
I know she's young, but you're nearby,
And I'll be near a phone."

Maybe did quite well;
She sat Alone upon the grouch
(By that, I mean she propped her
In the greenish-colored couch.)

Carefully, she used a spork
To feed Alone some goop.
(That is to say she gave her
What we call Gaspacho Soup.)

The venture was a great success,
So Alice and Tyrone
Thought, "Maybe Maybe's old enough
To tend Alone, alone."

THE SHOWER

It's known that in a shower,
    When the water's nice and hot,
Genius seems to blossom
    Out of ordinary thought.

When feeling warm and soapy,
    One is never at a loss
For clever things to say tomorrow,
    Talking to the boss.

A lot of brilliant thinking
    Has been done in this location.
This steam will clear my head,
    So I can deal—What in tarnation?

Dribble, surge and sputter?
    What's the matter with the tap?
This abominable shower
    Is a thinker's handicap!

Suddenly it's icy cold,
    Instead of warm, at all.
I'll never get the soap off,
    While I'm clinging to the wall!

Oh, no! It's shifting once again,
    From cold to super hot!
You see how my potential genius
    Always comes to naught?

LIVER PIE

Grass is purple,
Cows are plaid,
And tortoises can fly.
If you believe a word of that,
I'll eat a liver pie!

Bluebirds whinny,
Horses tweet,
And Jello doesn't quiver.
If you believe a . . . What? You do?
Then give me just a sliver.

NO BOSS

There is no Boss of Crayons
    Who will check on you and say,
"The law is: you must only color
    In a certain way!"
No "President of Perfect Pictures"
    Comes collecting fines
Or snatches off your paper,
    When you draw outside the lines.

AT THE GALLERY

A painting openly displays
    What occupies the mind
Of any artist, whether fame,
    Or love for humankind.

The scrutiny they undergo
    Can't help but make me wonder
Why some artists want to show
    What influence they're under.

A SEWING LESSON

We can whine to the people we know,
About problems that we undergo.
   Or else when our dreams
   Come apart at the seams,
Perhaps we could learn how to sew.

TOMATO SURPRISE?

"Betsy loved my Lemon Lush
    Recipe she tried.
Could you make a copy, Page?
    My hands are occupied."

"Sure. I'd love to do it, Mom,
    But what a drippy name!"
"Just invent another then,
    Since it'll taste the same."

When Page had finished writing it,
The former name was gone;
She chose a title she preferred,
    And quickly sent it on.

A few days later Betsy called,
    Sounding all confused.
"Is this the recipe I liked
    That had me so enthused?

"The word Tomato in the name
    Is puzzling, so I wish
You'd give some explanation for
This lemon-flavored dish!"

Page said, "A word like Lemon
    Was a dull way to begin it;
What makes it a Surprise,
    Is that there's no tomato in it!"

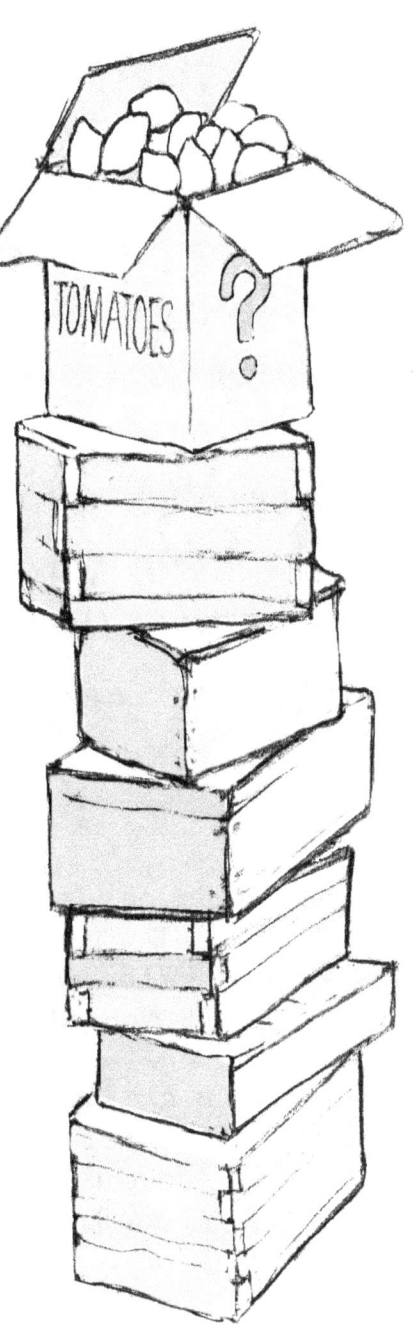

BETSY'S PEAR AMBROSIA
(Makes 8 Servings)

One can <u>pear halves</u>, largest size.
   (Or two, if they are small)
Take the baby off the counter,
   So she doesn't fall.

Dice the pears in one-inch bits.
   Don't cut the baby's hand.
Wipe her nose; give wooden spoon
   For drumming on a pan.

Scrape up <u>sour cream</u> from floor;
   Don't let it go to waste.
(For finger painting, try it mixed
   With red food-color paste)

Before she's pushed a chair nearby
   In hopes of climbing up,
Add remaining sour cream.
   You'll need about a cup.

One can <u>pineapple tidbits</u>, drained.
   Be sure to save the juice;
Put in baby bottle
   With a lid that isn't loose.

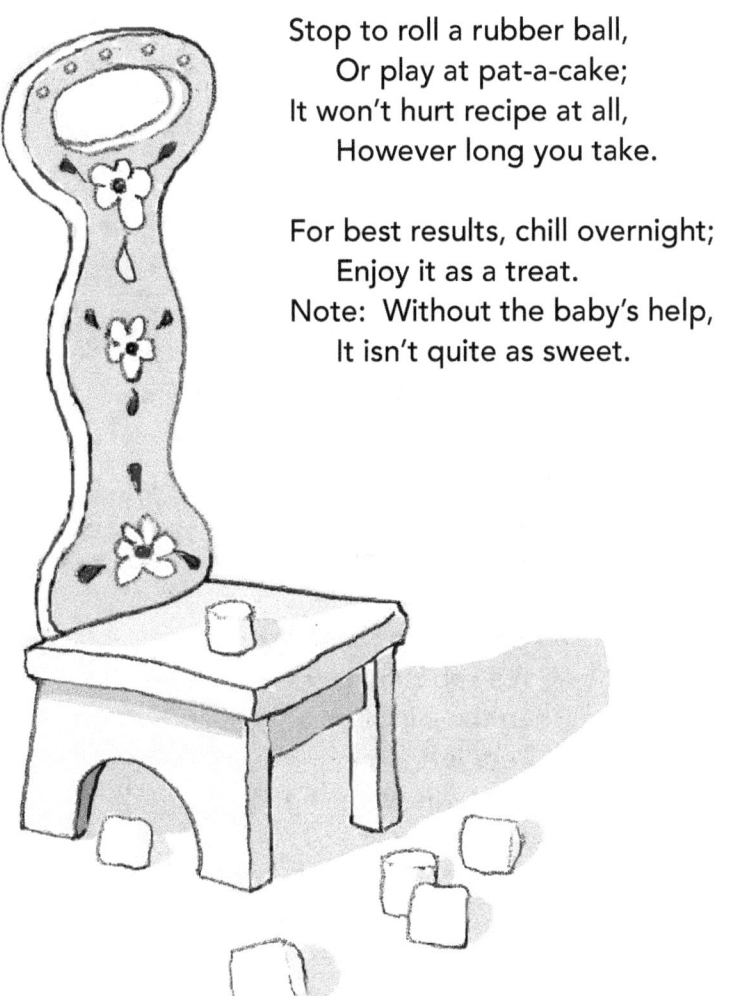

Large marshmallows (I use ten,
    Or possibly fifteen)
Don't worry if you're losing count,
    With kisses in between.

With scissors, snip them all in fourths;
    Don't use the mini size.
(It really makes a difference here,
    Not to compromise!)

Stop to roll a rubber ball,
    Or play at pat-a-cake;
It won't hurt recipe at all,
    However long you take.

For best results, chill overnight;
    Enjoy it as a treat.
Note: Without the baby's help,
    It isn't quite as sweet.

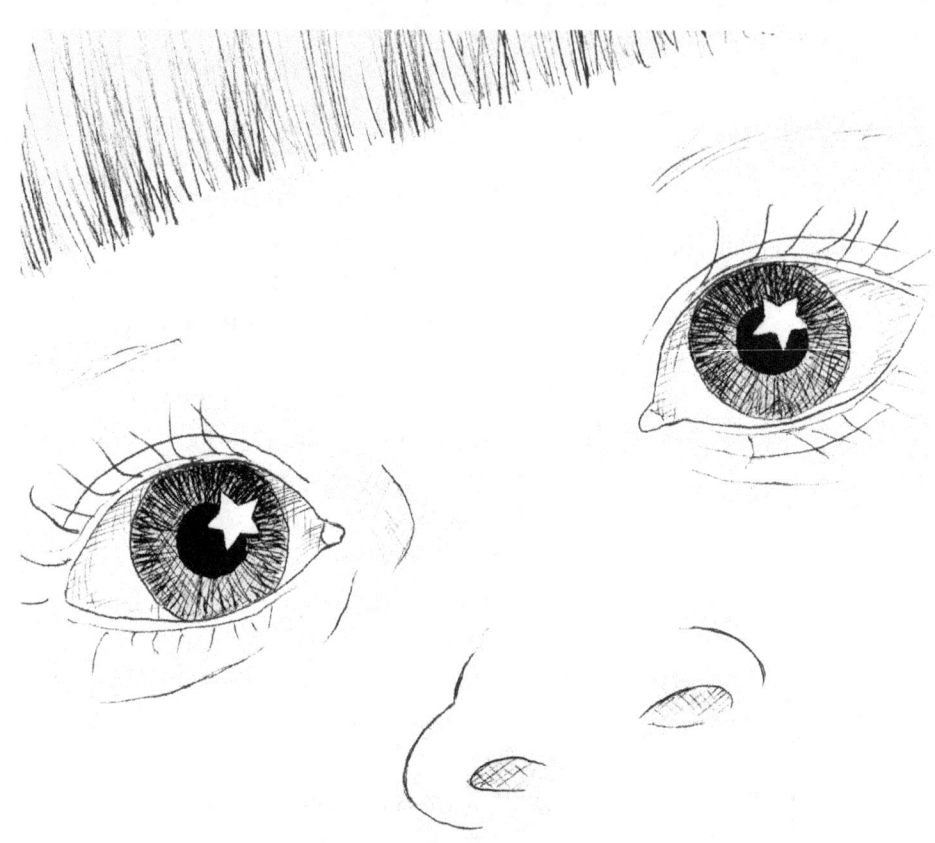

JANE MARTHA JANE

We know where you come from,
    but not how you came
Shining so brightly,
    Jane Martha, Jane!
Did you ride on the blaze
    of a shooting star,
When the windows of heaven
    were left ajar?
Tomorrow is watching
    for whatever lies
Awaiting the glow
    of your luminous eyes.

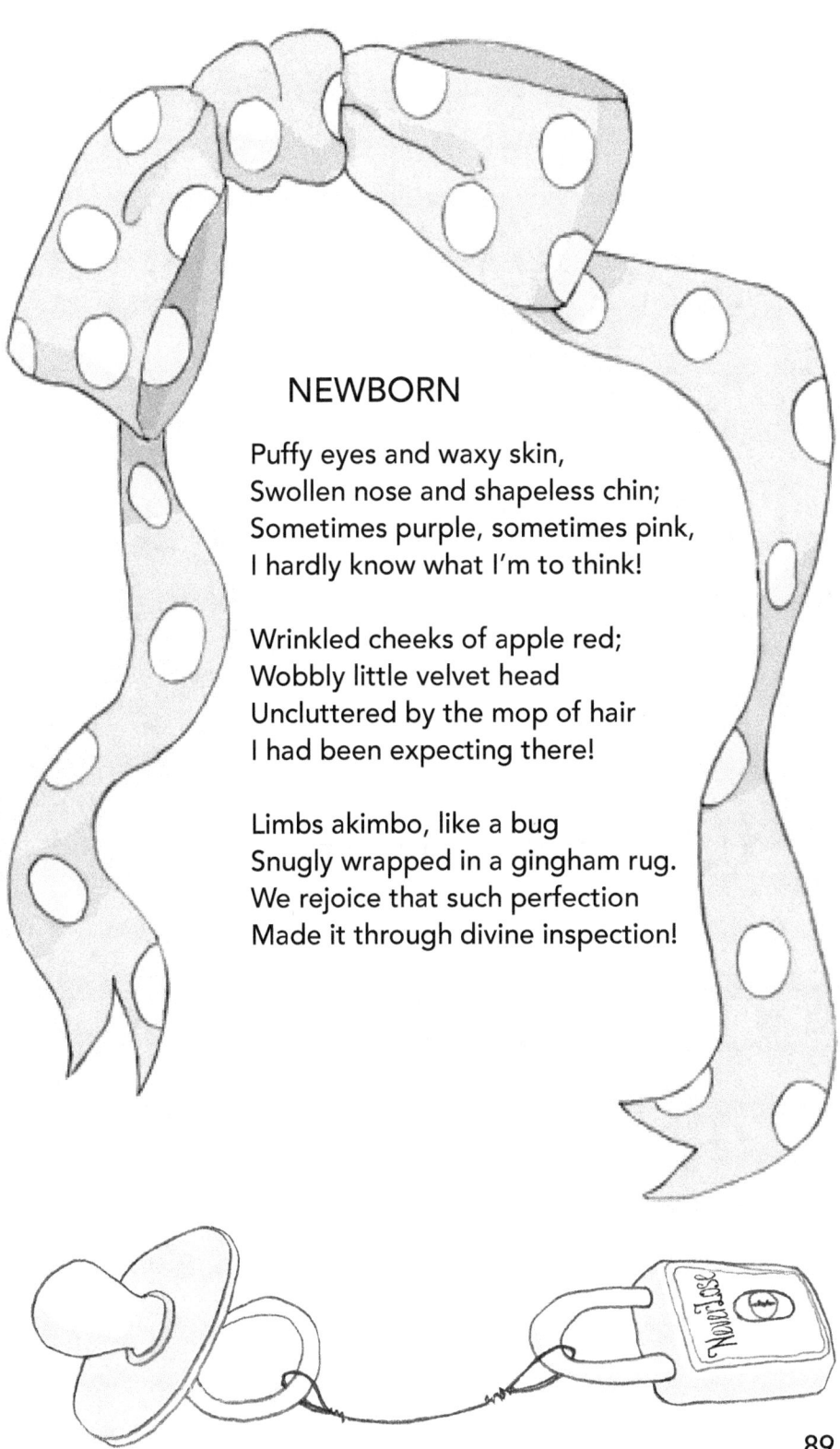

NEWBORN

Puffy eyes and waxy skin,
Swollen nose and shapeless chin;
Sometimes purple, sometimes pink,
I hardly know what I'm to think!

Wrinkled cheeks of apple red;
Wobbly little velvet head
Uncluttered by the mop of hair
I had been expecting there!

Limbs akimbo, like a bug
Snugly wrapped in a gingham rug.
We rejoice that such perfection
Made it through divine inspection!

FASHION STATEMENT

Looking sharp while acting rude
    Won't compensate for your attitude.
Of such, the evidence is ample;
    Look at Magpies, for example.
They're so mean, I'm unimpressed
    By the fancy way they're dressed.

DAYDREAM

I didn't have a puppy,
    So I dreamed a leather strap.
No rain for him to wander in?
    I dreamed a weather map.

Without a pair of wings,
    I dreamed a softly feathered cap
To fly him home and keep him where?
    Tethered to my lap!

But, real or not, I hope my dog
    Would like the kind of chap
Who'd toss him sticks,
    And fly with an imaginary strap.

To chase a dog through wind and rain,
    Who won't stay on my lap,
Has made me very tired,
    So I think I'll take a nap.

THOUGHTS WHILE BEING TUCKED IN BED

Mom can only rub my back
A minute, more or less;
I wish she'd write upon it
The Gettysburg Address.

THE TEA PARTY

Wade over the river to me;
It's only as high as your knee.
    If you can come over,
    We'll lie in the clover,
With thimbles of peppermint tea.

I will give you a sweet honeycomb,
And a daisy chain you can wear home.
    Though the river is high,
    You're not likely to die,
So we'll meet at the cherrywood throne.

SUMMER GUEST

We chirp and chatter gleefully,
    When you come home in May;
The blossoms help us make believe
    You're really here to stay!

Then, autumn nights, the chirping crickets
    Notify the flowers
That when you've said your fall farewell,
    The wilting will be ours.

 looks...

FRAFRIA (FRUH-FREE-UH)

We thought it would be better
    If the English alphabet
Had another letter,
    Not invented as of yet;
There ought to be a way to form
    All the words we need,
So we made up "Frafria,"
    Lest lack of it impede
Progress of the mother tongue
    And verbal self-expression.
(It seemed, when we were young,
    A meritorious obsession!)
We noticed yet another thing:
    All dictionaries lacked
The charming word FRAFRIA-FRING,
    Alarming in the fact
It is the only word to use
    The letter we invented,
A slight we thought we would excuse
    As long as they repented.

 ike

 ny

 quare

 entilated

 ox

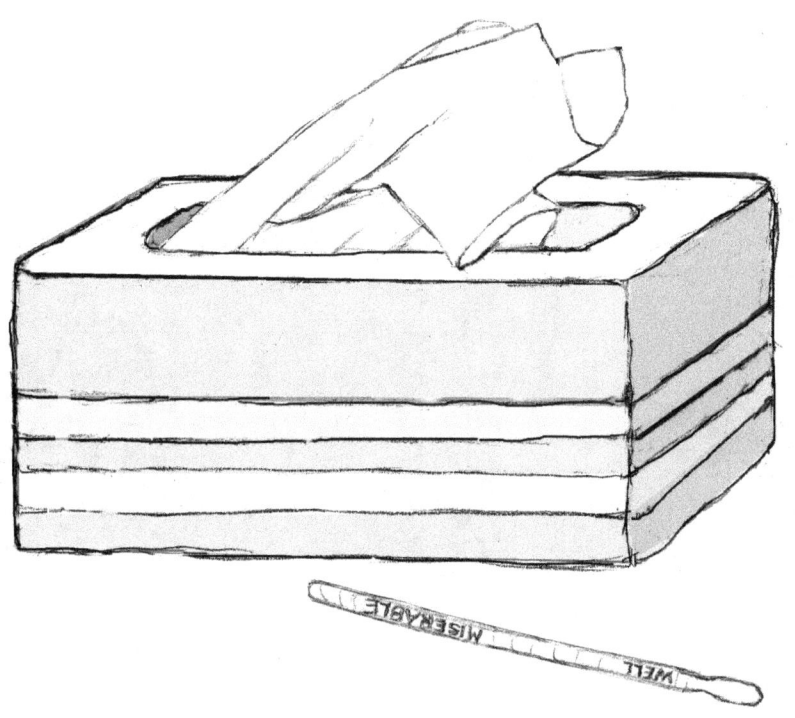

MEASLES START WITH ME

Purr is to persnickety
    What yell is to yellow.
So, concentrate and tell me
    What sell is to cellar.

Ink is to incredible
    As eggs are to exam.
Gull is heard in gullible,
    And amber starts with am.

Bedlam starts with bed.
    Also, truth to tell,
Measles start with me,
    And I don't feel so well.

GETTING EVEN

A scoop of ice cream ought to last
    Until your cake is gone.
The cake should be voluminous
    Enough to plop it on.

I don't much care if I get fat,
    I don't believe in leavin'
Some of this and some of that.
    They've got to come out even.

THE PARTY

I need to go on a diet.
Though they'll bring me ice cream pretty soon,
I won't be tempted to try it;
I'll settle for just a balloon!

However, I don't know why it
Would hurt to ask for a spoon.

IN THE MOONLIGHT

We drove to the hills
    To admire the moon,
Then we stood 'neath the stars,
    Until very soon
My heart skipped a beat,
    As he fell to his knees…
To search on the ground
    Where he'd dropped his keys.

UNCOMMITTED

They used to call him Bob
    ('cause it's the same when in reverse!)
And here's what I was thinking,
    as they took him in the hearse:

The art of indecision, he had carried to extreme:
    From the fifty-yard line, he cheered for either team.
    He couldn't quite decide what kind of music he preferred,
    And went until he died, without enjoying what he heard.

He never saw adventures, nor ever took a chance;
    In fact, he wore suspenders for fear he'd lose his pants.
His days were spent in waffling, unable to decide
    Anything as baffling as picking out a bride.

His favorite taste? Vanilla. His favorite color? Plaid.
    Nothing made him wildly happy. Nothing made him sad.
    How dull his life's rehearsal! But, wherever he has gone,
        He might make some reversal, and turn the music on!

    I pondered through his funeral
        (but never would have said):
    All the years I knew Bob,
        I thought that he was dead.

WISHING

When life has made us cry inside,
We wish it were pretend,
So we could tell the tale again,
Improving on the end.

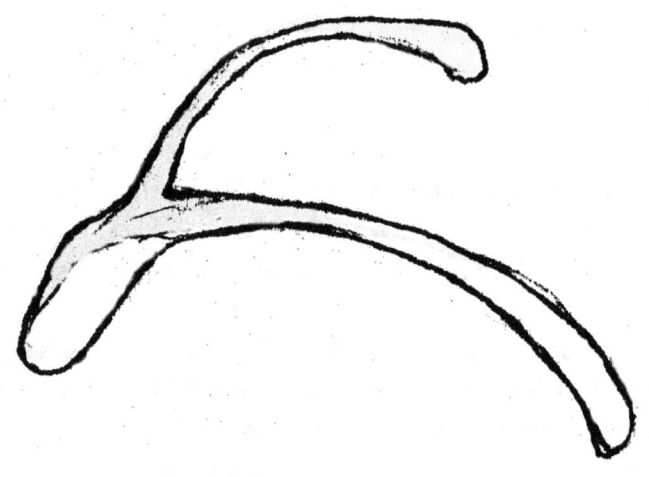

MEASURE UP

If you've got big shoes to fill,
Stand tall; adjust your glasses!
It means *prepare to measure up,*
Not *fill them with molasses.*

THE TREE

The old and weathered Oak Tree
    Is bending to the ground
So we can climb it easily,
    To see the world around.

JOYFUL READER

How joyfully my husband reads,
    When brandishing the pen he needs!
I really can't remember when
    He's read without a fountain pen;
Therefore, in our home, you'll find
    All the books are underlined.

MY FIELD TRIP REPORT

Whenever there's a speech I hear,
 With words both long and fancy,
My understanding of it all
 Gets just a little chancy.
But when I watched a lawyer man
 Perform before the court,
I learned some public speaking stuff,
 So here is my report:

 The lawyer spoke so nice and clear,
  Directing what he said
 Toward the jury member with the
  Least inside his head.
 When that one saw the light,
  He knew the rest could understand.
 So all the jury got the point,
  The way that he had planned!

  The lesson I have learned is this,
   As plain as it could be:
  To keep my speeches simple,
   And direct them just at me.
  So I don't speak to geniuses,
   Who make me feel inferior.
  I make perfect sense
   To my reflection in the mirror.

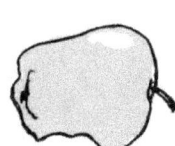

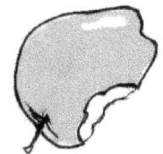

HAPPENMAKER

She looked so frail in the hospital bed,
    But she touched my hand and smiled,
Then asked, "Remind me, Dear,
    Are you my mother, or my child?

"I know! You are my Happenmaker,"
    She said, and laughed with pleasure.
I wish I'd told my mom
    It was a title I would treasure.

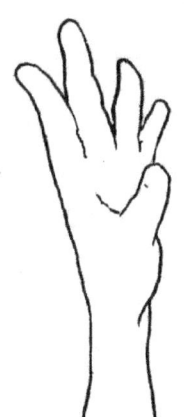
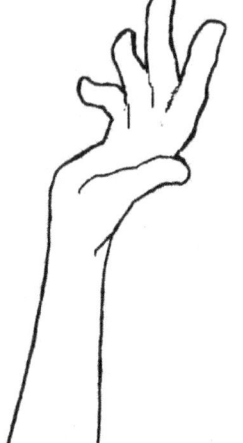

THEY WAIT

The love-worn bear, the sleepy mouse
    You thought were sent away
Still wait inside your memories,
    Until you want to play.

Why should you part with childish things?
    For even if you do,
Your fairies preen their dusty wings
    And fly back home to you.

AT THE REUNION

It's absolutely wonderful
    To see you once again!
How's your elbow doing?
    We really worried when
You had that run-in with the wall.
    It never did deter
You from working just as hard;
    How diligent you were!

Do your twins take after you,
    Or look more like their mother?
Did your sister win the car?
    And where's your younger brother?
We think of you with fondness,
    And hope you feel the same!
Here's hoping you'll forgive us,
    But we're groping for your name.

MEMORIES

My memories will never die,
    Nor ever be in short supply.
But if they start to peter out,
    I'll generate some more, no doubt.

PORTABLE FUN

Here's a rule I just made up:
   "No boredom is allowed,"
For each of us has got a head,
   In which there's room to crowd
Exciting things for later use,
   Like stories, thoughts and facts,
Providing entertainment,
   Which an empty noggin lacks.

THE LIST

Long ago I recognized
I ought to be more organized,
    and made a list;
I worked so very long and hard,
There's not a thing in that regard
    I could've missed!

I jotted down where I should go,
All the stuff I had to know,
    and so on.
I wrote the things I wanted done;
For every nine, I added one
    to grow on!

Don't ever make a list like mine
That eats up all your leisure time.
    Keep it short!
Or simply spread it on the bed
And beat it with a cane instead,
    for the sport.

Or make a paper airplane, then
Beat with gusto, once again.
    You won't regret it!
You know what I was forced to do,
When I saw how long it grew?
    Shred it!

It shouldn't be a big surprise
My organizing enterprise
    ended wrong.
I might have been a little wiser
To use my list as fertilizer,
    all along.

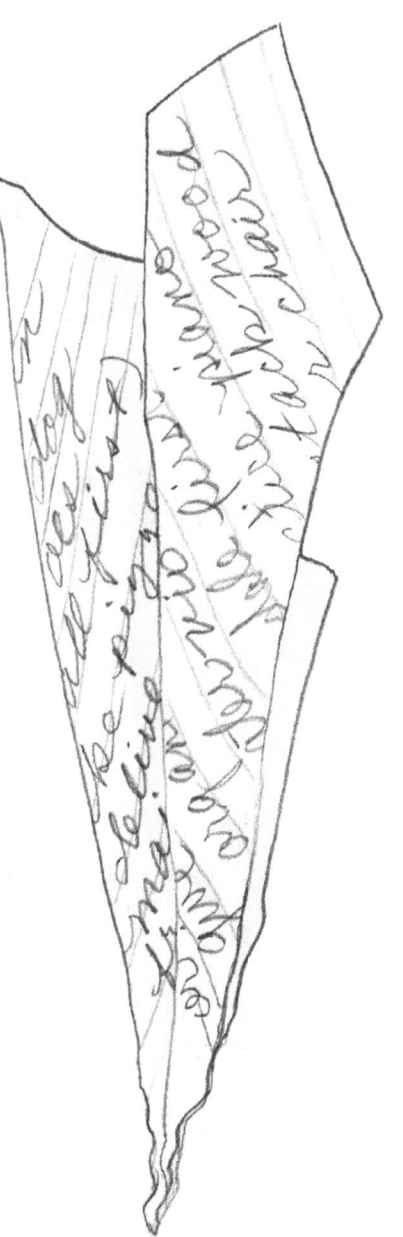

THE VALENTINE

He's missing arms and legs like ours,
    And many other parts.
But lest we feel superior,
    The earthworm has five hearts.

You'll get some pretty gifts with lace;
    The one from me has slime.
So here's my squirmy gift:
    A five times better Valentine!

MINIMALLY INVASIVE POSTERIOR LUMBAR DECOMPRESSION

A spineless sort of whimpering
    Was always on her lips.
From whence had come this jolting pain,
    In ankles, legs and hips?
When X-rays of a corkscrew
    Turned out to be her back,
Without another clue she figured,
    "Something's out of whack!"

Though deaf to talk of operations,
    By her own admission,
Good fortune smiled upon her,
    For she found a fine physician
Who made a slice and did a splice,
    Inside her ailing back.
In layman's terminology,
    He put it into whack.

Though nauseated briefly
    By what others thought was edible,
Nonetheless, she could report
    Her doctor was incredible.
Now she chortles gleefully,
    While sharing this impression
Of her very own Posterior
    Lumbar Decompression.

We now return with gratitude,
    To speak of Doctor Hooley,
Who fixed up that forementioned back
    Belonging to Yours Truly.

PLEASANTRIES

Did my "Hello, how are you?" sound empty,
    Like an old and tired joke?
If only you could hear my thoughts more clearly
    Than those simple words I spoke!

I like supposing that you understood me
    All the while:
I meant to say, "My world is brightened
    By your very smile."

SMILE

Be careful, as you speak Chinese,
    To use the proper tone;
You might say, "I'm a frog, please,"
    Instead of "Where's the phone?"
Or, "Eat a blue moustache today,"
    Instead of "Howdy-do."
But smile, whatever words you say,
    And they'll smile back at you.

CHANGE

There are things about myself
I ought to rearrange.
Instead, I shuffle furniture;
It's easier to change.

THE END

INDEX

A GENTLEWOMAN 60

A SEWING LESSON 84

A TAD 50

A MESSAGE TO ANONYMOUS 69

A WISE POINT 60

AN EAGLE 46

AND SYRUP 66

AT THE GALLERY 83

AT THE REUNION 105

BETSY'S PEAR AMBROSIA 86

BEWARE THE ATOMIZER! 13

BUTTERED TOAST 65

BY CAR 53

CHANGE 111

CRITTERS 7

DAYDREAM 91

DITTY SCHMITTY 56

DORIS AND THE CHORUS 56

FAIRY CHILD 55

FAREWELL 62

FASHION STATEMENT 90

FIDO FISH 70

FOREVERMORE 43

FRAFRIA 96

FROM DAD 71

GETTING EVEN 96

GONE 25

GOOSE ON THE LOOSE 6

GRANDMOTHER 64

HAPPENMAKER 103

HAPPY BIRTHDAY TO ME 68

I AM NOT A WIND-UP TOY 2

I AM WOMAN; HEAR ME SNORE 19

I CAN FLY 39

IN THE MOONLIGHT 98

INCOMPATIBLE GUESTS 11

INTRODUCTORY PIANO LESSON 26

JANE MARTHA JANE 88

JOYFUL READER 101

LAURA LEE 27

LITTLE TOMMY TOOTHPASTE 34

LIVER PIE 81

LOST EMAIL 28

LOST IN TRANSLATION 16

MAGIC 50

MAYBE AND ALONE 79

MEASLES START WITH ME 95

MEASURE UP 100

MEMORIES 105

MINIMALLY INVASIVE POSTERIOR
     LUMBAR DECOMPRESSION 109

MONKEY BUSINESS 49

MY BLACK HOLE 73

MY FIELD TRIP REPORT 102

MY MECHANICAL NOSE 10

NEW, EASY-OPEN CONTAINER 51

NEWBORN 89

NO BOSS 82

NO THANK YOU 72

NOT THAT BEDTIME STORY! 40

NOTE ON A CABIN DOOR 47

NOW THEY KNOW 15

ON FIRE 54

ONCE UPON A HAPPY TIME 37

OSTRICH OF THE IMAGINATION 6

PETS 9

PHOOEY 53

PLEASANTRIES 110

POETIC SENSE 3

PORTABLE FUN 106

PUPPY CARE 14

RHYME TIME 21

SMILE 110

SNOWFALL 77

SON 42

STEWED PRUNES 36

SUMMER GUEST 93

SUNRISE 32

SUPPERTIME 74

THE BEST CHRISTMAS 38

THE CHANGE OF PLANS 58

THE FATHER'S DAY GIFT 57

THE FISHERMAN 22

THE FLIGHT OF TIME 48

THE JUMPING BEAN 52

THE LATE SHOW 78

THE LIST 107

THE MEETING 43

THE PARTY 97

THE PLAYER PIANO 61

THE SHOWER 80

THE TEA PARTY 93

THE TREE 101

THE VALENTINE 108

THE WOOD 44

THEY WAIT 104

THOUGHTS OF LOST LOVE 45

THOUGHTS WHILE BEING
    TUCKED IN BED 92

TO A CLAM IN MY CHOWDER 77

TOMATO SURPRISE 85

UNCOMMITTED 99

VETERINARY EMERGENCY 8

VISITORS 30

WHAT NOT TO DO 29

WHAT YOU'LL NEED 67

WHO ATE MY CHAIR? 12

WHY WE EXERCISE 25

WISHING 100

YOUR CUP 20

www.ingramcontent.com/pod-product-compliance
Lightning Source LLC
Chambersburg PA
CBHW050559300426
44112CB00013B/1990